International Law and Sea Level Rise

The Law of the Sea

Volumes published in this Brill Research Perspectives title are listed at *brill.com/rpls*

International Law and Sea Level Rise

Report of the International Law Association Committee on International Law and Sea Level Rise

Edited by

Davor Vidas
David Freestone
Jane McAdam

BRILL

LEIDEN | BOSTON

This paperback book edition is simultaneously published as issue 2.3 (2018) of *Law of the Sea*, DOI:10.1163/24519359-12340006.

Library of Congress Control Number: 2019930465

Typeface for the Latin, Greek, and Cyrillic scripts: "Brill". See and download: brill.com/brill-typeface

ISBN 978-90-04-39818-4 (paperback)
ISBN 978-90-04-39819-1 (e-book)

This book is printed on acid-free paper and produced in a sustainable manner.

Contents

International Law and Sea Level Rise

Report of the International Law Association Committee on International Law and Sea Level Rise

Davor Vidas
Norwegian Branch of the International Law Association
dvidas@fni.no

David Freestone
British Branch of the International Law Association
davidacfreestone@gmail.com

Jane McAdam
Australian Branch of the International Law Association
j.mcadam@unsw.edu.au

Abstract

This issue contains the final version of the 2018 Report of the International Law Association (ILA) Committee on International Law and Sea Level Rise, as well as the related ILA Resolutions 5/2018 and 6/2018, both as adopted by the ILA at its 78th Biennial Conference, held in Sydney, Australia, 19–24 August 2018.

In Part I of the Report, key information about the establishment of the Committee, its mandate and its work so far is presented. Also, the background for the establishment of the Committee is explained, drawing on: (a) conclusions of the ILA Committee on Baselines and the related ILA Resolution 1/2012; (b) scientific assessments, such as by the Intergovernmental Panel on Climate Change (IPCC), regarding on-going sea level change and projections of future rise; and (c) more broadly, scientific findings regarding the profound changes taking place in the Earth system since the mid-20th century and predictions for their acceleration in the course of the 21st century. All of this has prompted the need, and provided the Committee with the relevant context, for the study of the options and elaboration of proposals for the development of international law.

Part II of the Report addresses key law of the sea issues through a study of possible impacts of sea level rise and their implications under international law regarding maritime limits lawfully determined by the coastal States, and the agreed or adjudicated

 | DOI:10.1163/9789004398191_002

maritime boundaries. This includes the study of the effects of sea level rise on the limits of maritime zones, and the analysis of the subsequently emerging State practice regarding the maintenance of their existing lawful maritime entitlements. The guiding consideration in developing the proposals and recommendations by the Committee for the interpretation and development of international law regarding the maritime limits and boundaries impacted by sea level rise has been the need to avoid uncertainty and, ultimately, facilitate orderly relations between States and contribute to the maintenance of international peace and security. A related ILA Resolution 5/2018 addresses maritime limits and boundaries impacted by sea level rise.

Part III of the Report addresses international law provisions, principles and frameworks for the protection of persons displaced in the context of sea level rise. The notion of 'human mobility' is used as an umbrella term that refers to all relevant forms of the movement of persons and, in the context of this report, covers displacement (which is forced), migration (which is predominantly voluntary), planned relocation and evacuations (which both may be forced or voluntary). This part of the report takes the form of principles entitled the 'Sydney Declaration of Principles on the Protection of Persons Displaced in the Context of Sea Level Rise' with commentaries. Accordingly, ILA Resolution 6/2018, which also contains the Sydney Declaration of Principles, addresses the protection of persons displaced in the context of sea level rise and contains recommendations by the Committee to this effect.

Keywords

sea level rise – climate change – law of the sea – maritime entitlements – maritime limits – maritime boundaries – human mobility – displacement – migration – planned relocation – evacuations

International Law Association Sydney Conference (2018): International Law and Sea Level Rise

Members of the Committee:

Professor Davor Vidas (Norway): *Chair*
Professor David Freestone (UK): *Co-Rapporteur*
Professor Jane McAdam (Australia): *Co-Rapporteur*
Dr Snjolaug Arnadottir (HQ)
Professor Vasco Becker-Weinberg (Portugal; *Nominee of Chair*)

Dr Markus Beham (Austria)
Professor Alan Boyle (UK)
Professor Elizabeth Burleson (USA)
Mr Bruce Burson (New Zealand)
Professor David Caron † (USA; *Nominee of Chair*)
Dr Chen-Ju Chen (China (Taiwan))
Professor Jean-Pierre Cot (France)
Professor Annie Cudennec (France)
Professor Maria Gavouneli (Hellenic)
Dr Antoine Grima (HQ)
Dr Daud Hassan (HQ)
Ambassador Marie Jacobsson (Sweden)
Alternate: Martin Ratcovich
Professor Walter Kälin (Switzerland; *Nominee of Chair*)
Professor Fernando Loureiro Bastos (Portugal)
Alternate: Professor Patricia Galvao Teles
Professor Charles Norchi (USA)
Alternate: Peter Prows
Dr Marcos Orellana (Chile)
Professor A G Oude Elferink (Netherlands)
Professor Alexander Proelss (Germany)
Professor Rosemary Rayfuse (Australia; *Nominee of Chair*)
Captain J Ashley Roach (USA)
Alternate: Dr Anita Halvorssen
Professor Shigeki Sakamoto (Japan)
Alternate: Jun Tsuruta
Professor Seokwoo Lee (Korea)
Professor Clive Schofield (Australia)
Alternate: Derek Tak Wei Wong
Professor Alfred H A Soons (Netherlands)
Dr Alejandra Torres Camprubi (Spain)
Professor Patrick H G Vrancken (South Africa)
Professor Maureen Williams (HQ)

REPORT (2018)

Part I: Background

A *Establishment of the Committee and Its Mandate*

The International Law Association (ILA) Committee on International Law and Sea Level Rise (hereinafter: Sea Level Rise Committee, or Committee) was established by the ILA Executive Council in November 2012.[1] The Committee was tasked with a two-part mandate:

(1) to study the possible impacts of sea level rise and the implications under international law of the partial and complete inundation of state territory, or depopulation thereof, in particular of small island and low-lying states; *and*

(2) to develop proposals for the progressive development of international law in relation to the possible loss of all or of parts of state territory and maritime zones due to sea level rise, including the impacts on statehood, nationality, and human rights.

The Executive Council appointed Professor Davor Vidas (Norwegian branch) as the Chair of the Committee, and Professors David Freestone (British branch) and Jane McAdam (Australian branch) as Co-Rapporteurs.[2] The Committee at present (8 June 2018) consists of 31 Members and six Alternates.

B *Background for the Establishment of the Committee*

When the proposal for the Sea Level Rise Committee was made in October 2012, it was prompted by the findings and conclusions of the ILA International Committee on Baselines under the International Law of the Sea (hereinafter: Baselines Committee), as contained in its report adopted at the 75th ILA Conference in Sofia, Bulgaria, in August 2012;[3] the discussions at the closed and open sessions of the Baselines Committee at the Sofia Conference;[4] and

1 ILA, *Minutes of the Meeting of the Executive Council* (London, 10 November 2012), at 5.

2 Ibid.

3 'Baselines under the International Law of the Sea: Committee Report', in: International Law Association, *Report of the Seventy-Fifth Conference held in Sofia, August 2012* (London: ILA, 2012), 385–428. Hereinafter: *Baselines Committee Sofia Report*. That report is available also on-line at ILA Baselines Committee webpage, at <www.ila-hq.org/en/committees/index.cfm/cid/1028>. In further references to that report below, page numbers indicated relate to the ILA printed published report version, and pages referred to in brackets relate to the on-line report version.

4 ILA, *Report of the Seventy-Fifth Conference held in Sofia, August 2012*, at 429–431 (regarding the record of the open session).

Resolution 1/2012 adopted at that conference.[5] The proposal for the Sea Level Rise Committee was also prompted by scientific findings regarding the profound changes taking place in the Earth system, especially since the mid-20th century. The prospect of accelerating changes in the course of this century, including sea level rise, will have consequent ramifications for the development of international law. This was the wider context motivating the proposal for a new ILA committee to focus on the international law implications of sea level rise.

1 Conclusions of the Baselines Committee Sofia Report and Resolution 1/2012

The first international committee of the ILA to study consequences of sea level rise as regards the implications for international law was the Baselines Committee, formed in 2008.[6] The Baselines Committee was established with a two-part mandate; as stated in the Committee's report, this was:

> first, to 'identify the existing law on the normal baseline' and, second, to 'assess if there is a need for further clarification or development of that law'. The need to identify, and possibly clarify or develop, the existing law concerning the normal baseline *arises in response to possible sea level rise* that has been predicted to accompany the phenomenon of climate change, and the effects this may have in particular upon low-lying, small island developing states.[7]

In its 2012 Sofia report, the Baselines Committee concluded:

> [I]f current predictions of sea level rise are realized, some States will become completely submerged. The resulting deterritorialization will likely mean, among other things, a total loss of baselines and of the maritime zones generated by coastal territory and measured from those

5 Ibid., at 17. Available also on-line at ILA Baselines Committee webpage, see at: <http://www.ila-hq.org/index.php/committees>.

6 The Baselines Committee was established by the ILA Executive Council in November 2008; see: ILA, *Minutes of the Meeting of the Executive Council* (London, 15 November 2008), at 4. The issue of sea level rise was later also touched upon by the ILA Committee on the Legal Principles Relating to Climate Change, in its Second Report (Sofia, 2012), at 29–30 and 39–40; text available at the ILA website.

7 *Baselines Committee Sofia Report* (n. 3), at 385–386 (on-line, at 1), referring to the *Proposal for the establishment of a new committee on baselines*, paras. 4 and 7; emphasis added.

> baselines. Should the issue of deterritorialization fall to be considered by the international community at least in part as a baseline issue, the existing law of the normal baseline does not offer an adequate solution. Here the Committee raises the possibility of deterritorialization in the context of Article 5 baselines, *but the loss of a State's territory to rising sea levels is not primarily a baseline or law of the sea issue*. Substantial territorial loss is a much broader issue encompassing concerns of statehood, national identity, refugee status, state responsibility, access to resources, and international peace and security. This issue requires consideration by a committee established for the specific purpose of addressing this range of concerns. The work of that committee should take into account the spirit of the modern law of the sea in which the interests of differently situated states are balanced. That committee should also recall the aims of the Convention: to strengthen peace, security, cooperation, and friendly relations among nations in conformity with the principles of justice and equal rights; to take account of the interests and needs of humankind as a whole; and to promote the economic and social advancement of all peoples of the world considering the special interests and needs of developing countries.[8]

Following on this, Resolution 1/2012 of the 75th ILA Conference recognised that:

> substantial territorial loss resulting from sea level rise is an issue that extends beyond baselines and the law of the sea, and encompasses consideration at a junction of several parts of international law, including such fundamental aspects as elements of statehood under international law, human rights, refugee law, and access to resources, as well as broader issues of international peace and security.[9]

The 2012 ILA Conference acknowledged that the issue requires consideration by a committee established for the specific purpose of addressing this broad range of concerns.[10]

---

8 *Baselines Committee Sofia Report* (n. 3), at 424–425 (on-line, at 30–31); emphasis added.
9 Resolution No. 1/2012, para. 7.
10 Ibid., para. 8.

2 Scientific Assessments of On-going Sea Level Change and Projections of Future Rise

As indicated above, it was new scientific evidence and findings that prompted the establishment of the Committee in 2012. These include in particular the findings of the Intergovernmental Panel on Climate Change (IPCC) concerning the trends in sea level change during the course of 20th century and the first decade of the 21st century, as well as its projections for further sea level rise. At the time of the establishment of this Committee in 2012, the IPCC had issued four assessment reports, the last of which was then published in 2007.[11] The Fifth Assessment Report (AR5)[12] of 2013/14, issued soon after this Committee was established, was the first to reverse a trend of successive reductions in the upper end of projections for 2100 in the previous IPCC reports. With an upper end prediction of 98 cm,[13] it is the second highest so far. Importantly, however, this prediction is based on major scientific advances since AR4, resulting in a better understanding of 20th century sea level change and its components, and in an improved ability to project future rise.[14] The AR5 also acknowledged, however, that significant challenges remain, in particular in incorporating the dynamics of the Greenland and Antarctic ice sheets.[15] The findings of the AR5 provide a major context for the work of this Committee, therefore the next three subsections briefly review the salient aspects of AR5: its progress in the

11 A brief overview of the previous four IPCC assessment reports, as related to sea level change, is found in: ILA, Interim Report of the Committee on International Law and Sea Level Rise, presented at the 77th ILA Conference, Johannesburg, August 2016 (hereinafter: *2016 Interim Report*), at 3–4; available online at: <http://www.ila-hq.org/index.php/committees>.

12 See especially J.A. Church et al., 'Sea Level Change', in: *Climate Change 2013: The Physical Science Basis. Contribution of Working Group I to the Fifth Assessment Report of the Intergovernmental Panel on Climate Change* (Cambridge University Press, 2013), (hereinafter: 'Sea Level Change', *Contribution of WG I to AR5*); *Climate Change 2014: Synthesis Report. Contribution of Working Groups I, II and III to the Fifth Assessment Report of the Intergovernmental Panel on Climate Change* (Core Writing Team, R.K. Pachauri and L.A. Meyer (eds)), IPCC: Geneva, 2015 (hereinafter: *AR5 – Synthesis*); and *Summary for Policymakers. In: Climate Change 2013: The Physical Science Basis. Contribution of Working Group I to the Fifth Assessment Report of the Intergovernmental Panel on Climate Change* (Cambridge University Press, 2013), (hereinafter: *AR5 – Summary for Policymakers*).

13 'Sea Level Change', *Contribution of WG I to AR5* (n. 12), at 1186. It is, moreover, noted that if the Antarctic precipitation increase is omitted from the process-based projections, the likely range increases to 103 cm; ibid.

14 'Sea Level Change', *Contribution of WG I to AR5* (n. 12), at 1204; also *AR5 – Synthesis* (n. 12), at 62.

15 *AR5 – Synthesis* (n. 12), at 56.

understanding of on-going sea level change; its improved projections of future sea level rise; and its analysis of the key challenges that remain.

2.1 *Progress in the Understanding of On-going Sea Level Change*

AR5 confirms that the amount of global mean sea level rise in the course of the 20th century and up to 2010 was ~20 cm.[16] A transition from relatively low mean rates of sea level change, that were characteristic for the previous two millennia (in the order of tenths of mm/year), occurred at some time between the end of the 19th to the early 20th century,[17] and led to higher rates of rise in the course of the 20th century (in the order of mm/year) – with a global mean rate of rise of 1.7 mm/year over the span of the century.[18] The key distinction observed in the course of the 20th century, as compared to previous centuries and even previous millennia, is not only the absolute amount of rise but also the accelerating rate of mean sea level rise that was noted, especially in measurements since 1971.[19] Between 1993 and 2010, the observed rate is already markedly greater: 3.2 mm/year.[20] This indicates both a greater amount of rise and an acceleration in the rate in the late 20th and the early 21st century.[21]

Current understanding of sea level rise identifies ocean thermal expansion and glacier melting (not including Antarctica) as the dominant contributors for most of the 20th century mean sea level rise; observations since 1971 result in estimates, with a degree of high confidence, that those two sources

16 That is: 0.19 [0.17 to 0.21, i.e., +/-0.02] m; 'Sea Level Change', *Contribution of WG I to AR5* (n. 12), at 1150.

17 AR5 refers to most recent studies concluding that sea level began to rise above the late Holocene background rate (characteristic of the previous ca 2000 years) between 1905 and 1945; 'Sea Level Change', *Contribution of WG I to AR5* (n. 12), at 1146 and 1184–1185.

18 'Sea Level Change', *Contribution of WG I to AR5* (n. 12), at 1146 and 1150, indicating the rate as 'very likely', meaning in AR5: 90 to 100 % probability; see also *AR5 – Summary for Policymakers* (n. 12), at 9.

19 Since 1971, significantly more ocean data became available and systematic glacier reconstructions began; global mean rate of sea level rise since 1971 was estimated to approximately 2.0 mm/year.

20 'Sea Level Change', *Contribution of WG I to AR5* (n. 12), at 1204, 1150; with the indication of this being 'very likely'. This rate is found by the satellite sea level altimetry data.

21 In this context, 1993 is also important as the first year when satellite sea level altimetry record, and observations of all sea level components, became available; a 20-year span (1993–2012) enabled trend analyses as presented in AR5; see *AR5 – Synthesis* (n. 12), at 41; 'Sea Level Change', *Contribution of WG I to AR5* (n. 12), at 1139 and, especially, at 1150. It is important to note here that satellite altimetry measures *sea surface height* (SSH), primarily in the open ocean, whereas tide gauges measure *relative sea level* (RSL) along the coastline. A change in RSL is the difference between the change in SSH and the vertical land motion. See also section I.B.2.3 below.

contributed about 75% of the observed rise.[22] However, the contribution of the Greenland and the Antarctic ice sheets to sea level rise has increased since the early 1990s.[23] AR5 indicates a progressive trend in which the Greenland contribution has 'very likely' increased from 0.09 mm/year (for 1992–2001) to 0.59 mm/year (for 2002–2011), while the Antarctic contribution 'likely' increased from 0.08 mm/year (for 1992–2001) to 0.40 mm/year (for 2002–2011).[24] This trend is significant for future projections, and it also poses important challenges for the (process-based model) projections, especially regarding the dynamical responses of the Antarctic ice sheet.

2.2 *Improvements in Projections of Future Sea Level Rise*

Confidence in the projections of global mean sea level rise has increased since the AR4, because of improved understanding of the physical components of sea level, the improved correlation between the process-based models and actual observations, and the inclusion of ice-sheet dynamical changes.[25] The projections of sea level rise contained in AR5 are larger than in AR4, primarily because of the improved modelling of land-ice contributions.

The projections of the likely amount of sea level rise in the 21st century range in AR5 from 26 cm rise at the lower-end of the lowest scenario (RCP2.6) to 98 cm rise at the upper-end of the highest scenario (RCP8.5).[26] The rate of rise, between 2081 and 2100, in the latter scenario is 8 to 16 mm/year.[27] This is, in the upper-end, a five-fold increase if compared with the rate of rise from 1993 to 2010, or almost ten times the average rate of rise (of 1.7 mm/year) in the 20th century.

Two additional aspects are estimated by AR5 as 'very likely' in the 21st century. First, that sea level change will have a *strong regional pattern*, with some places experiencing significant deviations of local and regional change, which

---

22 'Sea Level Change', *Contribution of WG I to AR5* (n. 12), at 1139 and 1157.

23 Ibid., at 1153–1157. Data for those contributions comes primarily from satellite and airborne surveys.

24 'Sea Level Change', *Contribution of WG I to AR5* (n. 12), at 1153. This translates into the average rate of ice loss from the Greenland, from 34 Gt/year (for 1992–2001) to 215 Gt/year (for 2002–2011), and from the Antarctic, from 30 Gt/year (for 1992–2001) to 147 Gt/year (for 2002–2011). As to contribution to global mean sea level rise: 100 Gt/year of ice loss is equivalent to 0.28 mm/year increase; *AR5 – Summary for Policymakers* (n. 12), at 7.

25 'Sea Level Change', *Contribution of WG I to AR5* (n. 12), at 1139.

26 Ibid., at 1180. 'Representative Concentration Pathways' (RCPs) are different future scenarios of concentration of greenhouse gases, aerosols, and other climate drivers. RCPs are dependent on human activities, technology and policy developments, yet these factors are not assessed in AR5.

27 Ibid., at 1180.

can differ from the global average rate by more than 100%; second, that there will be a significant increase in the occurrence of future sea level *extremes* in some regions (with a likely increase already in the early 21st century).[28]

While exact figures of amount and rates of future sea level rise still remain uncertain, even for the 21st century, AR5 states that it is 'virtually certain'[29] that sea level will continue to rise during the 21st century, and for centuries beyond – even if greenhouse gas (GHG) concentrations are stabilised (with the amount of rise in later centuries dependent on future GHG emissions).[30] For higher emission scenarios and warmer temperatures, surface melting of the Greenland ice sheet is projected to exceed accumulation, leading to its long-term decay and a sea level rise of several metres, consistent with paleo sea level data,[31] which indicates – for the last interglacial (between 129 and 116 thousand years ago) – between 5 and 10 m higher than the present-day global mean sea level that has been relatively constant for the last several thousand years.[32]

On current understanding, the only event that could cause global mean sea level to rise substantially above the *likely* range presented in AR5 during this century would be the collapse of the marine-based sections of the Antarctic ice sheet. However, the effect of this, which AR5 states 'cannot be precisely quantified', is, with *medium confidence*, predicted to be within several tenths of a meter of sea level rise during the 21st century.[33] The distinction between Antarctica and Greenland is that the latter has no known large-scale instabilities that might generate an abrupt increase in sea level rise.[34]

2.3 *Challenges that Remain*

It is clearly acknowledged in AR5 that significant uncertainties remain, particularly related to the magnitude and rate of the ice sheet contribution to sea level rise during the 21st century and beyond, as well as the regional

28 Ibid., at 1140.

29 In AR5 terminology of likelihood, 'virtually certain' means 99 to 100% probability.

30 'Sea Level Change', *Contribution of WG I to AR5* (n. 12), at 1205.

31 Ibid.

32 Ibid., at 1139 – implying, for estimates up to 10 m, substantial contributions from both the Greenland and the Antarctic ice sheets.

33 *AR5 – Synthesis* (n. 12), at 59; 'Sea Level Change', *Contribution of WG I to AR5* (n. 12), at 1140.

34 'Sea Level Change', *Contribution of WG I to AR5* (n. 12), at 1179. For further studies on the destabilisation of the West Antarctic ice sheet (especially around the Antarctic Peninsula and the Amundsen Sea area), see, e.g., C. Rye et al, 'Rapid sea-level rise along the Antarctic margins in response to increased glacial discharge' (2014) 7 *Nature Geoscience* 732–735, estimating that an excess of freshwater input of 430 (+/- 230) Gt/year is required to explain the observed sea level rise.

distribution of sea level rise and the regional changes in storm frequency and intensity.[35] AR5 states that:

> Although improved understanding has allowed the projection of a *likely* range of sea level rise during the 21st century, it has not been possible to quantify a *very likely* range or give an upper bound to future rise. The potential collapse of ice shelves, as observed on the Antarctic Peninsula (…), could lead to a larger 21st century rise.[36]

It should be added here that, regarding ocean warming, the AR5 predicts the most pronounced warming at greater depth in the Southern (Antarctic) Ocean. Recent studies, including those following the publication of AR5, have focused on the destabilisation of the West Antarctic ice sheet and its potential for contributing rapidly to global sea level rise.[37]

Another challenging aspect is the wide range of differences in the results for the upper bounds of projected sea level rise, identified in assessments using process-based modelling, on the one hand, and those based on semi-empirical models, on the other – with the latter resulting in upper bounds of up to 2.4 m of global mean sea level rise by 2100.[38]

A further important consideration is that of *relative* sea level rise, which is defined by the elevation of both the land and the sea. This concept acknowledges that as sea levels rise, complex feedbacks may occur on the shape or morphology of the coast as well as its associated systems (such as coral reefs) making some coasts highly responsive to changing sea levels.[39]

---

35 'Sea Level Change', *Contribution of WG I to AR5* (n. 12), at 1205.

36 Ibid., at 1205. In AR5 terminology of likelihood, 'likely' refers to a probability between 66 and 100% (while 'very likely' is 90 to 100 % probability).

37 See, e.g., Rye et al (n. 34). For highly relevant study supplementing the findings in AR5 see: R.M. DeConto and D. Pollard, 'Contribution of Antarctica to past and future sea-level rise' (2016) 531 *Nature* 591–597; A. Shepherd et al, 'Mass balance of the Antarctic Ice Sheet from 1992 to 2017' (2018) 558 *Nature* 219–222.

38 See 'Sea Level Change', *Contribution of WG I to AR5* (n. 12), at 1179–1186. The semi-empirical approach regards changes in sea level as an integrated response of the entire climate system, reflecting changes in the dynamics and thermodynamics of the atmosphere, ocean and cryosphere – in contrast to process-based approach, which explicitly attributes sea level rise to its individual physical components; ibid, at 1182.

39 Most studies on the resilience of low-lying coral atoll islands to sea level rise have projected that they will experience minimal inundation impacts until at least the end of the 21st century; a recent study, however, reports that these have not taken into account the additional hazard of wave-driven flooding on atoll infrastructure and impact on freshwater availability. See C.D. Strolazzi, S.B. Gingerich, A. van Dongeren et al, 'Most atolls will be uninhabitable by the mid-21st century because of sea-level rise exacerbating

Records of past sea level changes provide insights into the sensitivity of sea level to past climatic changes, and may also be able to contribute to our understanding of current changes and to provide a means of evaluating projections.[40] In contrast to the more recent gradual progressions of sea level rise that have occurred over a very long period, there is geological evidence of significant 'jumps' over a relatively short time-span of centennial – perhaps even decadal – scale,[41] followed by longer periods of general stability or slower rises. The timing of such future 'jumps' is very difficult to predict.

Discussing risk and the management of an uncertain future, AR5 states that – while it is 'unlikely' for global mean sea level rise to exceed one meter in this century – the consequence of a greater rise could be so severe that this possibility must become a significant part of risk assessment.[42] Relatively low confidence but high consequence outcomes are policy relevant – and therefore an aspect pertinent also in the considerations of the present Committee.

3 Change of Epochs in the History of the Earth: A New Context for International Law

The wider context for the proposal for this Committee were recent scientific findings regarding the profound changes that have been taking place in the Earth system, especially since the second half of the 20th century. The prospects of further and accelerated changes in the course of this century (reflected also in sea level rise) have possible ramifications for the development of international law. Scientific evidence increasingly indicates that, due to the nature and size of on-going and predicted changes, the Earth may already be undergoing a shift from the conditions of the current officially accepted geological time interval, the Holocene, to a new planetary state.[43] The Holocene is the latest, and formally still current, geological epoch, comprising the past 11,700

---

wave-driven flooding' (2018) 4 *Science Advances*, available online at: <http://advances.sciencemag.org/content/4/4/eaap9741>.

40 'Sea Level Change', *Contribution of WG I to AR5* (n. 12), at 1145 – confirming also that important progress has been made since AR4 in understanding the amplitude and variability of sea level during the past intervals when climate was warmer than pre-industrial.

41 See, e.g., M. O'Leary et al, 'Ice Sheet Collapse Following a Prolonged Period of Stable Sea Level during the Last Interglacial' (2013) 9 *Nature Geoscience* 796–800.

42 *AR5 – Synthesis* (n. 12), at 36.

43 See especially the review by 24 members of the Anthropocene Working Group: C. Waters et al, 'The Anthropocene is functionally and stratigraphically distinct from the Holocene' (2016) 351 *Science* 137; and, for the findings of the AWG so far see: J. Zalasiewicz et al, 'The Working Group on the Anthropocene: Summary of evidence and interim recommendations' (2017) 19 *Anthropocene* 55–60.

years,[44] marked especially during the last few thousand years by an exceptionally long period of relative environmental stability.[45] As such, the conditions of the Holocene were a key factor facilitating the development of human civilisation and, ultimately, the territorial divisions of the political world as we know it.

It has been argued that, because of the interaction between the global environmental effects of economic development and increased human population, the Earth system has already left the Holocene and has entered a new epoch: the Anthropocene.[46] So far, the 'Anthropocene' is an unofficial scientific term referring to the human imprint on the Earth system that is already so profound as to have reached geological significance.[47] Since 2009, the Anthropocene hypothesis is under formal scrutiny within geology: the Anthropocene Working Group (AWG) was set up then within the International Commission on Stratigraphy to examine the geological basis and the scientific justification for possible formalisation of the Anthropocene as the latest geological time unit.

The Holocene has been characterised, especially in its late stage, by the longest period of relatively stable temperate environmental and climatic conditions on Earth since the appearance of *Homo sapiens*. By contrast, the Anthropocene is seen as characterised by change, uncertainty, and instability in the future behaviour of the Earth system.[48] This may have increasing

---

44 M. Walker et al, 'Formal Definition and Dating of the GSSP (Global Stratotype Section and Point) for the Base of the Holocene Using the Greenland NGRIP Ice Core, and Selected Auxiliary Records' (2009) 24 *Journal of Quaternary Science* 3–17.

45 The lower boundary for the 'late Holocene' is currently proposed at 4200 years BP; see M. Walker et al, 'Formal subdivision of the Holocene Series/Epoch' (2012) 27 *Journal of Quaternary Science* 649–659.

46 On the onset of the Anthropocene, see: J. Zalasiewicz et al, 'When did the Anthropocene Begin? A Mid-Twentieth Century Boundary Level is Stratigraphically Optimal' (2015) 383 *Quaternary International* 196–203. For the origins of the Anthropocene hypothesis, see: P. Crutzen and E. Stoermer, 'The Anthropocene' (2000) 41 *Global Change Newsletter* 17–18; and P. Crutzen, 'Geology of Mankind' (2002) 415 *Nature* 23.

47 On the possible magnitude of that impact, see also a recent article in journal *Nature*: A. Ganopolski et al, 'Critical insolation-CO_2 relation for diagnosing past and future glacial inception' (2016) 529 *Nature* 200–203, reporting a modelling study confirming findings that the Earth would already be entering a new glacial interval (an 'ice age') absent human impact on the CO_2 concentration in the atmosphere from the 18th century on, and concluding that the onset of a glacial interval is, due to that impact, postponed by at least 100,000 years.

48 J. Zalasiewicz, P. Crutzen and W. Steffen, 'The Anthropocene', in F. Gradstein et al. (eds), *The Geologic Time Scale 2012*, Vol. 2 (Amsterdam: Elsevier, 2012), 1033–1040; and M. Williams et al, 'The Anthropocene Biosphere' (2015) 2 *The Anthropocene Review* 196–219.

relevance and, over time, important consequences for the organisation of international relations as currently regulated by international law.[49] It has been argued that within the current system of international law, the stability of the late Holocene has played a major role in the development of the political system which has in turn reflected the generally stable natural conditions of the Earth system.[50] Changes in that underlying element of stability contain the potential for new types of tension in relations between States.[51]

One such core aspect, which is in the focus of this Committee, relates to the international legal implications of sea level rise, as already projected for this century. The onset of changing Earth system conditions in an Anthropocene epoch may draw into question some key aspects of international law, since these rely on the general stability of geographic conditions, and may require the re-examination of some currently accepted paradigms of international law.

C *Work of the Committee and Focus of this Report*

After the establishment of the Committee at the end of 2012, its membership was initially appointed during the course of 2013. The first meeting of the Committee was held at the 76th ILA Conference, in Washington DC, in April 2014.[52] Three main issue-areas to be dealt with by the Committee were defined at that meeting: the law of the sea; forced migration and human rights; and issues of statehood and international security. Although each of these issue-areas has already attracted a lot of research and publications, the Committee considered that it could make a useful contribution, within the framework of its mandate, by synthesising these various issues, elaborating interlinkages and considering options for proposals *de lege ferenda*.

The Committee agreed to divide its work thematically into two main stages and to first focus on priority areas in a relatively shorter-term perspective. This involved two parallel streams of study: one on the law of the sea issues and the other on the migration and human rights issues. The second stage would then follow and involve the study of the statehood question and other issues of

49 D. Vidas, J. Zalasiewicz and M. Williams, 'What is the Anthropocene – and Why Is It Relevant for International Law?' (2015) 25 *Yearbook of International Environmental Law* 3–23.

50 D. Vidas et al., 'International Law for the Anthropocene?' (2015) 9 *Anthropocene* 1–13.

51 Ibid.

52 See ILA, *Report of the Seventy-Sixth Conference, held in Washington D.C., April 2014* (London: ILA, 2014), at 877–881. At the time of the 76th Conference, the Committee had 21 members and 4 alternates. Two-thirds of the members (14 out of the 21) took part. Minutes of the sessions (open and closed), held on 9 and 10 April 2014, are available at: <http://www.ila-hq.org/index.php/committees>.

international law and international security prompted by the mid- and longer-term predictions of sea level rise.

The Committee presented its Interim Report at the 77th ILA Conference, held in Johannesburg, in August 2016.[53] The Interim Report, as it was agreed, was not fully comprehensive and was limited to an overview of the two streams of study identified above. This Report follows up and elaborates on the 2016 Interim Report and presents proposals by the Committee for the development of international law in the two identified fields of study. The two Resolutions, proposed by the Committee and adopted by the ILA Assembly at the 78th ILA Conference in Sydney in August 2018 as Resolutions 5/2018 and 6/2018, are appended.

To facilitate the work of the Committee between the biennial ILA Conferences, three intersessional meetings were held: first, in Oslo, Norway, 12–13 June 2015, organised and hosted by the Fridtjof Nansen Institute, FNI (attended by 16 members); second, at Lopud, Croatia, 15–16 September 2017, organised and hosted by the FNI and TBA21 Foundation (attended by 20 members); and third, in Singapore, at the National University of Singapore, 15 March 2018 (attended by 10 members).

Regarding the third study area comprised by its mandate, concerning the statehood question and other issues of international law and international security prompted by the partial or complete inundation of State territory or the depopulation thereof, the Committee was aware of the mid- and longer-term perspective involved. In view of the broad and complex scope of its mandate, the Committee agreed not to continue further discussion of these issues for the purposes of this Report. The Committee considered that it would be useful to continue its work beyond the present term in 2018, by extending its mandate to enable a closer focus on these fundamental issues as well as other related matters, including especially transitional issues and how to deal with diminishing statehood as a process.[54]

Part II: Law of the Sea Issues

This part of the Committee's Report addresses key law of the sea issues that are raised by both parts of its mandate, i.e., regarding the *study* of the 'possible impacts of sea level rise and the implications under international law',

53 The *2016 Interim Report* (n. 11).

54 See further discussion in section II.B, below.

and in connection with *developing proposals* 'for the progressive development of international law'.

In its Interim Report, submitted to the Johannesburg ILA Conference in 2016, the Committee reviewed the issues identified by the Baselines Committee in its 2012 Sofia Report and discussed the legal issues raised by the impacts of relative sea level rise on coasts and coastal basepoints. In the 2016 Interim Report, the Committee had also reviewed the existing literature in order to identify a number of possible approaches *de lege ferenda* to the issues that the impacts raise.

A *Sea Level Rise and Maritime Zones and Boundaries*

As already outlined in Part I above, and in further detail in the Committee's 2016 Interim Report,[55] the IPCC in AR5, revising the predictions in AR4, posits global mean sea level rise of up to approximately one metre by 2100. According to scientific reports issued since AR5, this may ultimately prove to be a conservative estimate. Moreover, AR5 suggests that sea level rise is likely to exhibit 'a strong regional pattern, with some places experiencing significant deviations of local and regional sea level change from the global mean change'.[56] One metre of change in sea level may pose potentially serious, maybe even disastrous, threats to many coastal States, especially those with large, heavily populated and low-lying coastal areas, as well as for small, low-lying island States. Such sea level change is also highly likely to impact coastal areas where wetlands and other sites may be protected by international treaty regimes,[57] although the highly variable responses of different coastal environments to changing sea levels also need to be taken into account.

In addition to the threat posed to low-lying coastal areas and their associated populations, as well as to coastal infrastructure from inundation by rising seas, there are also threats to the ocean spaces adjacent to such threatened territories. In particular, sea level rise has the potential to impact significantly the spatial extent of national claims to maritime jurisdiction.[58]

---

55 See the *2016 Interim Report* (n. 11), 3–7.

56 'Sea Level Change', *Contribution of WG I to AR5* (n. 12), at 1140.

57 Under, e.g., the 1971 Ramsar Convention on Wetlands of International Importance, 996 UNTS 245; (1972) 11 ILM 963; as well as under regional conventions.

58 The literature on this is extensive. Early (legal) writers agreed that this was a consequence of ambulatory baselines: E. Bird and J. Prescott, 'Rising Global Sea Levels and National Maritime Claims', (1989) 1 *Marine Policy Reports* 177–196; A.H.A. Soons, 'The Effects of a Rising Sea Level on Maritime Limits and Boundaries', (1990) 37 *Netherlands International Law Review* 207–232; D.D. Caron, 'When Law Makes Climate Change Worse: Rethinking

Generally, the baseline from which States' maritime zones are measured is the 'normal' baseline, determined in accordance with Article 5 of the 1982 United Nations Convention on the Law of the Sea (LOSC), as the low-water line along the coast.[59] From this baseline, States may measure their territorial sea,[60] contiguous zone,[61] exclusive economic zone (EEZ)[62] and continental shelf.[63] Consequently, if the 'normal' baseline moves inland as a consequence of sea level rise, so too will the outer limits of those maritime zones measured from such baseline, if the basepoints that control the definition of the outer limits to maritime zones are impacted. As a result of such shifting baselines and the consequential adjustments of the outer limits of maritime zones, waters previously under national jurisdiction could become part of the high seas (or become part of the EEZ rather than the territorial sea). Moreover, changes to the baselines could impact upon maritime boundaries between States with opposite or adjacent coasts.

Further, sea level rise has the potential to inundate small islands and other geographical features which may have generated their own maritime zones,[64] or been used by the coastal State as basepoints, including for drawing straight baselines.[65] This too may have major impacts on the capacity of a feature to generate maritime jurisdictional claims.[66] Loss of such small

the Law of Baselines in Light of Rising Sea Level' (1990) 17 *Ecology Law Quarterly* 621; D. Freestone, 'International Law and Sea Level Rise' in: R.R. Churchill and D. Freestone (eds), *International Law and Global Climate Change* (London/Dordrecht: Graham and Trotman/Martinus Nijhoff, 1991), 109, 119–122; D. Freestone and J. Pethick, 'Sea Level Rise and Maritime Boundaries: International Implications of Impacts and Responses', in: G. Blake (ed.) *International Boundaries: Fresh Perspectives*, Vol 5 (Routledge, 1994), 73–90.

59 Article 5 of the 1982 United Nations Convention on the Law of the Sea, UN Doc. A/CONF.62/122; text in 1833 UNTS 3; text reprinted in (1982) 21 ILM, at 1261; available at <www.un.org/Depts/los>.

60 Article 3, LOSC.

61 Article 33, LOSC.

62 Article 57, LOSC.

63 Article 76(1), LOSC. Of course, defining the outer limit of the continental shelf is more complex as the continental shelf extends beyond a coastal State's territorial sea 'throughout the natural prolongation of its land territory to the outer edge of the continental margin', and therefore for many coastal States it extends beyond 200 nautical miles from the baselines.

64 Article 121, LOSC.

65 As permitted by Article 7, LOSC.

66 See generally the detailed provisions of Part II, LOSC. For example, the low-water line of islands may be used to measure maritime zones (Article 121(2)). The low-water line of low-tide elevations (LTE) may also be used to measure maritime zones if the LTE is situated 'wholly or partly at a distance not exceeding the breadth of the territorial sea

islands or other features as basepoints may be particularly crucial for archipelagic States. Article 47 of the LOSC lays down strict criteria for the drawing of archipelagic baselines and the loss of key basepoints may mean that the remaining basepoints are further apart than the Convention permits or the resulting water-to-land ratio no longer meets the necessary requirements.[67] Such changes would affect maritime zone claims but might also even compromise the State's ability to maintain its claim to archipelagic status. Although it is generally accepted that coastal States may undertake physical measures to maintain their existing baselines, it was recognised that for many coastal States this would not be a feasible option due to the costs involved.

As the discussion in Part III of this Committee's 2016 Interim Report demonstrates, some low-lying island States, already under pressure, may find their land area rendered uninhabitable well before they are overrun by the sea.[68] In extreme cases this will raise questions as to the ability of some island States to maintain their statehood without a habitable land area, and to maintain sovereignty over the territorial sea, and consequently their sovereign rights over the resources of the maritime zones appurtenant to those land areas.[69]

The Sea Level Rise Committee had decided that in its 2018 Report it would consider how international law may be able to respond to these unprecedented existential challenges as well as the serious human dimension of the issues. In particular, the Committee was concerned with the two questions flagged by the Baselines Committee in its 2012 Sofia Report – namely the effect of sea

---

from the mainland or an island' (Article 13(1), LOSC). All these features are susceptible to change.

67 Article 47(1): 'An archipelagic State may draw straight archipelagic baselines joining the outermost points of the outermost islands and drying reefs of the archipelago provided that within such baselines are included the main islands and an area in which the ratio of the area of the water to the area of the land, including atolls, is between 1 to 1 and 9 to 1'. Article 47(2): 'The length of such baselines shall not exceed 100 nautical miles, except that up to 3 per cent of the total number of baselines enclosing any archipelago may exceed that length, up to a maximum length of 125 nautical miles'.

68 See the *2016 Interim Report* (n. 11), 20–22.

69 This may include the resources of the 200 nautical mile EEZ in which coastal States have 'sovereign rights for the purpose of exploring and exploiting, conserving and managing the natural resources, whether living or non-living, of the waters superjacent to the sea-bed and of the sea-bed and its subsoil' (Part V, LOSC), and of the continental shelf over which coastal States exercise 'sovereign rights for the purpose of exploring it and exploiting its natural resources' (Part VI, LOSC). See also R. Rayfuse, 'Sea Level Rise and Maritime Zones: Preserving the Entitlements of "Disappearing" States' in: M.B. Gerrard and G.E. Wannier, *Threatened Island Nations: Legal Implications of Rising Seas and a Changing Climate* (Cambridge Univ Press, 2013), 167–191.

level rise on the outer limits of maritime zones and the effects of coastline changes on maritime boundaries.[70]

The Baselines Committee had concluded that, as a matter of international law, 'the normal baseline is ambulatory' and that consequently 'if the legal baseline changes with human-induced expansions of the actual low-water line to seaward, then it must also change with contractions of the actual low-water line to landward'.[71] The Baselines Committee therefore took the view that

> ... the existing law of normal baseline applies in situations of significant coastal change caused by both territorial gain and territorial loss. Coastal states may protect and preserve territory through physical reinforcement, but not through the legal fiction of a charted line that is unrepresentative of the actual low-water line.[72]

Consequently, the Baselines Committee concluded that

> ... extreme circumstances [landward changes of the baseline] could result in total territorial loss and the consequent total loss of baselines and of the maritime zones measured from those baselines. The existing law of the normal baseline does not offer an adequate solution to this potentially serious problem.[73]

The Baselines Committee had recommended 'that the issue of impacts of substantial territorial loss resulting from sea level rise be considered further by a Committee established for the specific purpose of addressing the wide range of concerns it raises'.[74] This, therefore, was the wider issue and the finding *de lege lata* that the Baselines Committee passed on to this Committee for further study and for the formulation of proposals *de lege ferenda*. In considering the implications of the findings by the Baselines Committee, the Sea Level Rise Committee decided to address two important preliminary issues that the Baselines Committee had identified in its 2012 report, namely:

> negative impacts on maritime boundaries negotiated in reliance on normal baselines in existence at the time of a delimitation, and the outer

70 Those questions were preliminarily surveyed by the Committee in the *2016 Interim Report* (n. 11), 12–18.

71 *Baselines Committee Sofia Report* (n. 3), at 422 (on-line, at 28).

72 Ibid., at 424 (on-line, at 30).

73 Ibid., at 426 (on-line, at 31).

74 Ibid., at 426 (on-line, at 31).

limits of a State's maritime zones proclaimed in reliance upon a normal baseline.[75]

1 Effects of Sea Level Rise on Limits of Maritime Zones

The 2016 Interim Report summarised the key issue as follows:

When sea levels rise, the low-water line along the coast – which marks the 'normal baseline' for the purposes of Article 5 – will usually move inland and some key geographical features used as basepoints for delineating the outer limits of maritime zones and for the delimitation of maritime boundaries may be inundated and lost. If, as a matter of international law, the normal coastal baseline is ambulatory (as the Baselines Committee has concluded),[76] then in situations where a baseline moves inland[77] and critical basepoints from which maritime zones are measured are inundated, the outer limits of the maritime zones which are measured from this baseline may also move landward.[78] In situations where key geographical features which are used as basepoints for the construction of baselines are totally inundated, these movements landward may be even more substantial. This same principle of course applies to the archipelagic baselines of archipelagic States, where the effect of losses of key basepoint features may result in pronounced changes in maritime entitlements, including the potential invalidation of archipelagic baselines systems.[79] Although small island States are likely to be the most obviously affected by such changes, the Committee felt it important to note that these changes would be likely to affect many, if not most, coastal States.

After reviewing the literature (discussed in the 2016 Interim Report) at its Oslo Intersessional Meeting in June 2015, two general approaches *de lege ferenda* to this issue had been identified by the Committee:

---

75 Ibid., at 422–423 (on-line, at 29). Regarding those issues, the Baselines Committee considered that 'under these circumstances [of the prospect of significant sea level rise], a question arises as to whether the existing law of normal baselines would or should apply'; ibid., at 432 (on-line, at 29).

76 Ibid., at 426 (on-line, at 31).

77 Also, note that because of changes in sediment flows rising sea may in some circumstances also have an opposite effect in some places – accreting sediments to push the low-water line seaward.

78 Where the outer edge of the natural prolongation of the continental shelf is less than 200 nautical miles from the coastal baseline, then the outer limit of the shelf may extend to 200 nautical miles from the baseline (Article 76(1), LOSC). Due consideration should be here given also to Article 76(9) LOSC, which states that the 'coastal State shall deposit with the Secretary-General of the United Nations charts and relevant information, including geodetic data, permanently describing the outer limits of its continental shelf'.

79 See Article 47, LOSC.

a) The first approach would be to propose that coastal States maintain (or 'freeze') their existing baselines, established in accordance with the LOSC, in their current position, as marked on 'large scale charts officially recognised by the coastal State',[80] or through the definition of baselines by other appropriate means such as the definition of geographical coordinates, notwithstanding physical changes in coastline and basepoints brought about by sea level rise;
b) The second approach would be to propose that coastal States maintain their existing defined outer limits of their maritime zones measured from baselines established in accordance with the LOSC, notwithstanding physical changes in the coastline and basepoints brought about by sea level rise.

At the 2016 Johannesburg ILA Conference, it was felt that the issue would benefit from wider discussion within the Committee. An extended discussion was then held at the Lopud Intersessional Meeting in 2017, as thoroughly documented in the minutes of that meeting.[81] It was pointed out that the Committee's proposals on freezing of maritime zones would constitute a derogation from the LOSC, and that the option of freezing baselines implied possible breaches of the law of the sea on the landward side of the territorial sea whereas the option of freezing the outer limits of maritime zones implied possible breaches on the seaward side of the territorial sea.[82]

Subsequently, at the Singapore Intersessional Meeting, held in March 2018, it was suggested that the use of the term 'freezing' was misleading, and that more appropriate terminology would be 'maintaining existing entitlements' to maritime zones – whether that was done by maintaining existing baselines drawn in accordance with the requirements of LOSC or by maintaining the outer limits of the territorial sea, EEZ or the continental shelf, all provided that these had been delineated in accordance with LOSC.

In developing these options, the Committee was at pains to point out that it was highlighting possible, not mandatory action by coastal States. It also appreciated that each of the above options might involve a change in the

80 Article 5, LOSC. Note there is no requirement in the LOSC for the coastal State to notify these 'normal baselines'. Article 16 LOSC appears only to require coastal State to give 'due publicity' to such charts when baselines, or the limits derived therefrom, are 'determined in accordance with articles 7, 9 and 10'.

81 See *Minutes of the Inter-sessional Meeting of the ILA Committee on International Law and Sea Level Rise, held at Lopud, Croatia, 15–16 September 2017*, available at the ILA webpages, at: <www.ila-hq.org/index.php/committees>.

82 Ibid., at 14–15.

current interpretation of the rules of the LOSC as applied to such situations. If the coastal State were to maintain the baseline that it had determined in accordance with the LOSC, even after physical changes to its coastline and maybe the loss of small off-shore features, then it could find itself with a claimed baseline that did not reflect reality. It might also find itself maintaining claims to off-shore territorial sea areas for which the physical justification had disappeared, unless it were able to afford to build artificial structures on these features in order to maintain their viability as basepoints. That requirement would be an expensive course of action that would excessively penalise the poorest and most vulnerable States. The issue may arise, for example, if low-tide elevations within the original territorial sea had become completely submerged,[83] or if offshore islands, claiming a full suite of maritime zones as permitted by Article 121(2) LOSC, became 'rocks' for the purposes of Article 121(3),[84] or even became low-tide elevations 'situated at a distance exceeding the breadth of the territorial sea' from the actual coastline.[85] For archipelagic States, this could also become complicated as the rules for the drawing of archipelagic baselines set out in Article 47 LOSC require a series of basepoint requirements and some complex calculations.[86] For example, the submergence of a feature or features and thus the elimination of one or more critical basepoints defining the system of archipelagic baselines leading to a redefinition of the baselines system may mean that the system no longer fulfils the land-to-water ratio test set out in Article 47(1).[87]

If on the other hand a coastal State maintained its existing entitlements to maritime zones by utilising the existing defined outer limits of its maritime zones measured from baselines established in accordance with the LOSC, then if the baseline retreated or crucial baseline features were lost, the concept of the ambulatory baseline might mean that the distance between the new baseline and the outer limit might exceed 12 and 200 nautical miles for the territorial sea, and the EEZ and continental shelf (for narrow-margined States), respectively.[88]

---

83 So that their use as 'the baseline for measuring the breadth of the territorial sea', under Article 13(1) LOSC, would be lost.

84 I.e., they became unable to support human habitation or a life of their own as result of loss of area or elevation.

85 Article 13(2), LOSC.

86 E.g., the requirements of Article 47(1); see text in n. 67, above.

87 See Article 47(1), LOSC.

88 See Article 57, LOSC: 'The exclusive economic zone shall not extend beyond 200 nautical miles from the baselines from which the breadth of the territorial sea is measured'.

The Committee agreed that its proposals regarding the legal consequences of sea level changes expected in the near future should seek to minimise proposed changes to the settled law of the sea. The Committee therefore took the view that the most important consideration at this stage was that its proposals should as far as possible attempt to reduce legal uncertainties regarding maritime boundaries and the limits of maritime zones at a time when many coastal States are facing the challenges of sea level rise impacts. In particular, the Committee's proposals should aim to facilitate orderly relations between States and, ultimately, the avoidance of conflict – bearing in mind that one of the principal motivations of the LOSC is to contribute to the maintenance of peace.[89] In the light of these considerations, the Committee identified the key arguments for and against the two approaches discussed briefly above.

i) *Maintaining Baselines despite Physical Changes Brought about by Sea Level Rise*

Maintaining existing baselines would mean that, if there were landward movement of the low-water line and loss of basepoints from which the baseline was measured, the baseline would nevertheless remain the same as officially promulgated earlier in accordance with the requirements of the LOSC. This would mean that, in the case of mainland coasts, the area of internal waters landward of the promulgated baseline, which is usually shallow and often non-navigable, would increase. It could also mean – as discussed above – that the coastal State could find itself with a charted baseline that did not reflect reality and might also find itself maintaining claims to offshore territorial sea areas for which the hitherto physical terrestrial justification had become submerged.

The arguments in favour of such an approach include the following:

- The coastal States' charts that define their baselines and their maritime zones would remain in force and would not require the reassessment and recharting that might be required by the effects of ongoing sea level change; alternatively, other appropriate means of defining baselines could be employed such as the use of geographical coordinates rather than the use of nautical charts, something that is already evident from State practice;
- Coastal States would retain their existing entitlements to maritime zones of the widths prescribed by the LOSC, notwithstanding the loss of territory and/or basepoints;

89 See Preamble to the LOSC, especially the first and seventh preambular paragraphs.

- Perverse incentives to artificially preserve baselines and basepoints that might otherwise become invalid under the current law of the sea regime would be removed;
- The current exclusive authority (sovereignty) of the coastal State over its territory would be maintained, recognising that the mix of the land and internal waters within that area has shifted;
- The status quo regarding the allocation of national maritime zones and common spaces under the law of the sea that has occurred on the basis of the existing law – assuming no sea level rise – would be maintained;
- Continuation of existing obligations under international law with respect to particular ocean areas would be safeguarded;
- Coastal and island States would be shielded from some of the adverse impacts of climate change, to which few contributed.

The arguments against such an approach include the following:

- If a coastal State were to maintain a chart showing a legal baseline which no longer reflects the position of the actual low-water line, then this would be a legal fiction and, according to the conclusions of the Baselines Committee that, as a matter of international law, the normal baseline is ambulatory, a breach of that rule;
- Coastal States may find themselves with offshore areas of territorial sea or even EEZs where the physical features which generated those maritime zones have submerged or, because of rising sea level, have ceased to retain the characteristics required by the LOSC to be fully-entitled 'islands' under Article 121(1);
- Coastal States would still need to update their navigational charts, even though the charts representing the legal baseline might remain the same; otherwise the legal fiction might pose risks to safety of navigation. The ongoing updating of charts is, however, an existing obligation for the purposes of ensuring safety of navigation, as IHO guidelines suggest charts should always show the limits of the territorial sea and the EEZ, based on the previously drawn baseline;
- It could be argued that by maintaining existing baselines, coastal States were preventing high seas areas from expanding, and preventing territorial sea areas from becoming EEZ, and this might be seen as contrary to a global public interest, in that these new high seas areas would be subject to high seas freedoms (some of which apply within the EEZs too).

ii) *Maintaining Existing Outer Limits despite Physical Changes Brought about by Sea Level Rise*

Maintaining existing entitlements would mean that once the coastal State has determined the outer limits of its territorial sea, EEZ or the continental shelf in accordance with the LOSC, and deposited the appropriate charts and/or geographical co-ordinates with the UN Secretary-General, then it does not have to change those outer limits notwithstanding any physical changes to its baseline or basepoints that may arise through sea level rise.

The arguments in favour of this approach include the following:

- Coastal States would retain their existing charted maritime zones and claims to maritime spaces beyond the outer limits of the territorial sea;[90]
- It would remove the perverse incentive to artificially maintain physical features to preserve maritime zone entitlements;
- The baseline would move (probably landward) to reflect the physical reality of sea level rise (i.e., it would remain ambulatory) in compliance with international law;
- The coastal States navigational charts would reflect the actual coastline and important features – so mariners would be aware of changes;
- Coastal (including island) States would be shielded from these adverse impacts of climate change, to which few contributed.

The arguments against include the following:

- Maintaining the declared outer limits while allowing the baseline to change or recede would mean that the breadth of a coastal State's maritime zones might exceed the 200 nautical miles from the baselines limit set by the LOSC;
- Maintaining only the outer limits of the EEZ and continental shelf would result in different implications for the outer limits of the territorial seas, which then might move dependent on the changes of baselines;
- Mariners would need to continue to be aware that the area of territorial sea of the coastal State might change;
- As with the maintaining of baselines above, it could be argued that maintaining outer limits in this way is preventing high seas areas from expanding and this might be seen as contrary to a global public interest.

---

90 For the continental shelf, this practice would be in conformity with Article 76(9) LOSC which provides for 'permanently describing the outer limits of the continental shelf"; see also footnote 78 above.

Other relevant considerations raised by the Committee included concerns about the status of existing excessive maritime zone claims or of baseline claims that did not comply with the LOSC. Here the Committee recognised that there were existing procedures for States to protest and object to maritime claims which are not in compliance with the LOSC requirements. Although these procedures would continue to exist the Committee took the view that its recommendations regarding the maintenance of existing entitlements were based on the premise that the coastal State's existing maritime claims were in compliance with the requirements of the LOSC and have been duly published or notified to the UN Secretary-General as required by the relevant provisions of the LOSC.[91]

Questions were also raised as to whether these claims could be maintained as a permanent solution or only a temporary one. It was thought that this should depend upon the ultimate objective of any proposed solution, which is to facilitate legal certainty as well as to facilitate orderly relations between States and contribute to the avoidance of conflicts.

A further issue of which the Committee was aware was the fact that its recommendations must have practical utility and clarity for coastal and island States facing the impacts of sea level rise and for international courts and tribunals that might in the future be called upon to decide disputes arising out of such changes.[92]

Concern was also raised about the impact of suggested proposals *de lege ferenda* on the principle that the 'land dominates the sea'. Some Committee

---

91 Namely, Article 5 regarding due publicity of normal baselines on 'large-scale charts officially recognized by the coastal State'. Charts or lists of geographical co-ordinates showing baselines measured under Article 7, 9 and 10 must be deposited with the UN Secretary-General under Article 16(2), as well as those regarding archipelagic baselines (under Article 47(9)), regarding EEZ outer limits (Article 75(2)) and regarding continental shelf outer limits (Article 76(9)).

92 In the *Bay of Bengal* maritime boundary arbitration (*Bangladesh v. India*), Bangladesh argued that the potential effects of sea level rise in the Bay of Bengal will be that 'within a few years' the low-tide elevations chosen by India would be likely to change or disappear, and that even the coastal locations of the basepoints chosen by Bangladesh might well be submerged. In the view of the Tribunal, this argument was not relevant; as the Tribunal stated: 'The issue is not whether the coastlines of the Parties will be affected by climate change in the years or centuries to come. It is rather whether the choice of basepoints located on the coastline and reflecting the general direction of the coast is feasible in the present case and at the present time'. Referring to a previous judgment of the International Court of Justice (*Black Sea*, 2009), the Tribunal stressed that it is concerned with the 'physical reality at the time of the delimitation'. See *The Bay of Bengal Maritime Boundary Arbitration* (*Bangladesh v. India*), PCA Case 2010–16, Award of 7 July 2014, paras 213–215.

members pointed out that the phrase 'the land dominates the sea' does not appear in the LOSC and that it is essentially a pragmatic judge-made axiom for use in maritime delimitation disputes and not necessarily relevant to the current situation.[93] Other Committee members considered the scope and impact of the 'land dominates the sea' principle as of far broader reach under the general law of the sea, beyond being limited to international jurisprudence reflecting it.[94] It was felt that it would be useful for the Committee in its future work to set out the origins, scope, and current application of this principle and to consider the legal consequences of its application in the context of the impacts of sea level rise. The Committee agreed that a paper should be developed on the principle that 'the land dominates the sea' as a part of the further work by the Committee.

1.1 *Emerging State Practice*

The Committee noted with considerable interest the emerging and important body of regional practice within the Pacific region. On 16 July 2015, seven leaders of Polynesian States and Territories signed the Taputapuātea Declaration on Climate Change at Papeete, in Tahiti. This Declaration by Polynesian leaders was made in advance of the Twenty-first Session of the Conference of the Parties to the UN Framework Convention on Climate Change (UNFCCC COP 21) in Paris. It states:

---

93 Caron has called it the 'vestigial remnant of the naturalist position that the existence of land is the source of authority over the ocean'; see D.D. Caron, 'Climate Change, Sea Level Rise and the Coming Uncertainty in Oceanic Boundaries: A Proposal to Avoid Conflict', in: S-Y. Hong and J.M. Van Dyke (eds), *Maritime Boundary Disputes, Settlement Processes, and the Law of the Sea* (Boston: Brill/Martinus Nijhoff, 2009), 1, 14.

94 A well-known formulation of this view has been the one by Prosper Weil: 'From the moment States were recognised as having rights over areas of sea ... these rights have been based on two principles which have acquired an almost idiomatic force: the land dominates the sea and it dominates it by the intermediary of the coastal front'; see P. Weil, 'Geographic Considerations in Maritime Delimitation', in: J.I. Charney and L.M. Alexander (eds), *International Maritime Boundaries*, vol. 1 (Dordrecht: Nijhoff, 1993), at 115, drawing on: P. Weil, *The Law of Maritime Delimitation – Reflections* (Cambridge University Press, 1989), at 50. See also discussion by D. Vidas, 'Sea Level Rise and International Law: At the Convergence of Two Epochs' (2014) 4 *Climate Law* 70–84, at 72–75; and, in a broader context, D. Vidas, 'International Law at the Convergence of Two Epochs: Sea Level Rise and the Law of the Sea for the Anthropocene', in: H.N. Scheiber, C. Esposito, J. Kraska and M-S. Kwon (eds), *Ocean Law and Policy: 20 Years under UNCLOS* (Leiden and Boston: Brill/Nijhoff, 2017), 101–123. See also the discussion in: *ILA Committee on International Law and Sea Level Rise: Minutes of the Open Session, Johannesburg, 10 August 2016*, available at the ILA website, at: <www.ila-hq.org/index.php/committees>.

> [T]he Polynesian Leaders Group call upon all State Parties to the UNFCCC to …
>
> **With regard to the loss of territorial integrity:**
>
> – Accept that climate change and its adverse impacts are a threat to territorial integrity, security and sovereignty and in some cases to the very existence of some of our islands because of the submersion of existing land and the regression of our maritime heritage.
>
> – Acknowledge, under the United Nations Convention on the Law of the Sea (UNCLOS), the importance of the Exclusive Economic Zones for Polynesian Island States and Territories whose area is calculated according to emerged lands and permanently establish the baselines in accordance with the UNCLOS, without taking into account sea level rise.[95]

More recently, in March 2018 eight Pacific island leaders attending the second Leaders' Summit of the Parties to the Nauru Agreement (PNA) signed 'The Delap Commitment on Securing Our Common Wealth of Oceans – reshaping the future to take control of the fisheries'.[96] The Signatories acknowledged the importance of regional co-operation and also acknowledged:

> The challenges presented by their unique vulnerability and the threat to the integrity of maritime boundaries and the existential impacts due to sea level rise.

To that end they agreed:

> To pursue legal recognition of the *defined baselines* established under the United Nations Convention on the Law of the Sea to remain in perpetuity irrespective of the impacts of sea level rise.[97]

A practical example from the region is provided by the Republic of the Marshall Islands which on 18 March 2016 passed comprehensive new legislation,

---

95 Signed by the leaders of French Polynesia, Niue, Cook Islands, Samoa, Tokelau, Tonga and Tuvalu. Text at: <http://www.presidence.pf/files/Polynesian_PACT_EN_15-07-15.pdf> (last accessed 8 June 2018).

96 The Commitment was signed in Majuro in the Marshall Islands on 2 March 2018 by the heads of State or their representatives of The Federated States of Micronesia, Republic of Kiribati, Republic of the Marshall Islands, Republic of Nauru, Republic of Palau, Independent State of Papua New Guinea, Solomon Islands and Tuvalu.

97 Ibid., para. 8; emphasis added.

repealing 'in its entirety' the 1984 Maritime Zones Declaration Act, and declaring anew all its maritime zones.[98] Freestone and Schofield have pointed out that this Marshall Islands action represents one of the latest developments in an emerging pattern of practice in the Pacific region whereby States are unilaterally declaring and publicising their maritime jurisdictional baselines, limits and boundaries. While stability in the spatial scope of a State's maritime jurisdiction has clear administrative as well as enforcement benefits, the wider implication of this practice is that it appears to be a deliberate attempt to pre-empt arguments that physical changes to its coastline, particularly those resulting from climate change induced sea level rise, would have resulting impacts on its baselines and/or on the outer limits of its zones.[99] Similar legislation, designating new archipelagic waters and designating the outer limits of the national EEZs has also been passed by Kiribati[100] and Tuvalu.[101]

This practice is, moreover, in keeping with, and was foreshadowed by, a strategy document developed by the Pacific Island Forum called the *Framework for a Pacific Oceanscape*,[102] whose Strategic Priority 1 concerns jurisdictional rights and responsibilities. That document urges, in Action 1A, that the Pacific Island Countries and Territories (PICTs) should, 'in their national interest', deposit with the UN coordinates and charts delineating

98 Act No. 13 of 2016. Source at: <http://www.un.org/depts/los/LEGISLATIONANDTREATIES/PDFFILES/DEPOSIT/mhl_mzn120_2016_1.pdf>. Discussed in detail by D. Freestone and C. Schofield, 'Republic of the Marshall Islands: 2016 Maritime Zones Declaration Act: Drawing Lines in the Sea' (2016) 31 *International Journal of Marine and Coastal Law* 720–746.

99 This and the following section draw on Freestone and Schofield (n. 98).

100 Baselines around the Archipelagos of Kiribati Regulations, 2014, at: <http://www.un.org/depts/los/LEGISLATIONANDTREATIES/PDFFILES/KIR_2014_archipel_baselines_regulations.pdf>. Also Kiribati Exclusive Economic Zone Outer Limit Regulations, 2014, available at: <http://www.un.org/depts/los/LEGISLATIONANDTREATIES/PDFFILES/KIR_2014_eez_outer_limits_regulations.pdf>; cited by S. Kaye, 'The Law of the Sea Convention and Sea Level Rise after the *South China Sea* Arbitration' (2017) 93 *International Law Studies*, at 444.

101 Declaration of Archipelagic Baselines 2012, LN No. 7 of 2012 (Tuvalu), <http://www.un.org/depts/los/LEGISLATIONANDTREATIES/PDFFILES/tuv_declaration_archipelagic_baselines2012_1.pdf>.

102 See C. Pratt and H. Govan, *Our Sea of Islands, Our Livelihoods, Our Oceania. Framework for A Pacific Oceanscape: a catalyst for implementation of ocean policy* (Pacific Islands Forum Secretariat, November 2010), available at: <http://www.forumsec.org/wp-content/uploads/2018/03/Framework-for-a-Pacific-Oceanscape-2010.pdf> (last accessed 8 June 2018). See also useful background and summary of the Pacific Boundaries Project provided by R. Frost, P. Hibberd, M. Nidung, E. Artack, M. Bourrel, 'Redrawing the Map of the Pacific', *Marine Policy* (In press, corrected proof, available online 21 June 2016: <https://www.sciencedirect.com/journal/marine-policy/articles-in-press>.

their maritime zones.[103] Action 1B, entitled 'Regional Effort to Fix Baselines and Maritime Boundaries to Ensure the Impact of Climate Change and Sea Level Rise Does Not Result in Reduced Jurisdiction of PICTs', states explicitly:

> Once the maritime boundaries are legally established, the implications of climate change, sea level rise and environmental change on the highly vulnerable baselines that delimit the maritime zones of Pacific Island Countries and Territories should be addressed. This could be a united regional effort that establishes baselines and maritime zones so that areas could not be challenged and reduced due to climate change and sea level rise.[104]

So, there is at least *prima facie* evidence of the development of a regional State practice in the Pacific islands – many of which are the most vulnerable to losses of territory and, consequently, baseline points from sea level rise. The Pacific island States would of course be among those 'States whose interests are specially affected', a significant attribute regarding the establishment of a general practice in the formation of a new rule of customary international law, as recognised by the International Court of Justice in the *North Sea Continental Shelf* cases.[105] The emergence of a new customary rule will require a pattern of State practice, as well as *opinio juris*. The Committee was conscious of the fact that the recommendations in its 2018 Report, if they were discussed and approved by the political organs of the UN, might well contribute to the formation of that *opinio juris*.

1.2 *Proposal of the Committee*

The Committee then considered the question of how it might present any proposal *de lege ferenda* that coastal and island States should have the option to maintain their maritime entitlements notwithstanding changes brought about by sea level rise. In its 2016 Interim Report, the Committee had referred to the options discussed by Hayashi (some of which he admitted might not be practical).[106] These included the development of customary international

103 See the *Framework*, in Pratt and Govan (n. 102) at 57.

104 Ibid., at 58.

105 *North Sea Continental Shelf Cases* (*Federal Republic of Germany/Denmark; Federal Republic of Germany/Netherlands*), Judgment, [1969] ICJ Reports, paras 73–74.

106 See the *2016 Interim Report* (n. 11 above), at 15.

law,[107] a protocol to the UN Framework Convention on Climate Change,[108] utilisation of the amendment provisions of the LOSC,[109] a decision of the Meeting of the State Parties to the LOSC (SPLOS),[110] a diplomatic conference open also for States non-parties to the LOSC, or an agreement adopted by the UN General Assembly after negotiation in its subsidiary bodies or informal consultations.[111]

The Committee noted the considerable legal and political complexities involved in a number of these options, including particularly the amendment procedure outlined in the LOSC itself. It then considered the mechanics of the evolution of a new rule of customary international law and also considered whether any proposals it might make on this issue could be influential in the contemporary interpretation of the text of the LOSC. In particular, its attention was drawn to the work of the International Law Commission regarding 'subsequent practice' in relation to the work of the Commission regarding interpretation of treaties under the 1969 Vienna Convention on the Law of Treaties.[112] Article 31(3)(b) of the Vienna Convention envisages that, in interpreting treaties, 'any subsequent practice in the application of the treaty which

107 As suggested by Soons in 1990 (n. 58), at 255.

108 As proposed in 1990 by the Coastal Zone Management Subgroup of the IPCC, reported by Freestone and Pethick (n. 58), at 76.

109 See Articles 311–316, LOSC. For a discussion of the complexity of this procedure see, e.g., D. Freestone and A.G. Oude Elferink, 'Flexibility and Innovation in the Law of the Sea: Will the LOS Convention Amendment Procedures Ever Be Used?' in A.G. Oude Elferink, (ed.), *Stability and Change in the Law of the Sea: The Role of the LOS Convention*, (Boston/Leiden, Nijhoff, 2005) 163–216.

110 Note that Article 319(2)(e) LOSC appears to allocate only administrative roles to this meeting, e.g. under LOSC Annex II, art 293 and Annex VI, arts 4(4), 18 and 19, discussed in Freestone and Oude Elferink (n. 109), 207–209.

111 All discussed further by M. Hayashi, 'Sea Level Rise and the Law of the Sea – Future Options', in: D. Vidas and P.J. Schei (eds), *The World Ocean in Globalisation: Climate Change, Sustainable Fisheries, Biodiversity, Shipping, Regional Issues* (Boston/Leiden: Brill/Martinus Nijhoff, 2011) 197, 200–206.

112 *Report of the International Law Commission: Sixty-eighth session* (2 May–10 June and 4 July–12 August 2016) A/71/10.118 at 121. Chapter VI, on Subsequent agreements and subsequent practice in relation to the interpretation of treaties. Conclusion 4. Definition of subsequent agreement and subsequent practice: …

> 2. 'subsequent practice' as an authentic means of interpretation under article 31, paragraph 3(b), consists of conduct in the application of a treaty, after its conclusion, which establishes the agreement of the parties regarding the interpretation of the treaty.
>
> 3. Other 'subsequent practice' as a supplementary means of interpretation under article 32 consists of conduct by one or more parties in the application of the treaty, after its conclusion.

establishes the agreement of the parties regarding its interpretation' shall be taken into account, together with the context.[113]

The Committee recognised that there were a number of procedural options open to States that wished to take advantage of its proposals and, while deciding not to propose any specific option at this point, expressed the hope that a Resolution of the International Law Association might be the most effective first step in bringing its recommendations to a wider audience. It noted the strong evidence of emerging State practice in the Pacific region regarding the intent of many island States to maintain their maritime entitlements in the face of sea level rise. The Committee took the view that, if it were to make recommendations regarding the maintenance of maritime entitlements, these should be global not regional – as they would need to be opposable to the world community, not *inter se* limited to the States of a particular region. Its proposal was also premised on that fact that there was, in the short term, unlikely to be a different solution agreed upon by the States on a global basis.

The Committee therefore recommends that a proposal be put together in a Resolution of the International Law Association proposing that States should accept that, once the baselines and the outer limits of the maritime zones of a coastal or an archipelagic State have been properly determined in accordance with the detailed requirements of the 1982 Law of the Sea Convention, that also reflect customary international law, these baselines and limits should not be required to be readjusted should sea level change affect the geographical reality of the coastline.

The Committee considered that this proposal should remain unchanged as long as there is no different solution agreed upon in a universal, globally applicable treaty.

---

113 Article 31(2) and (3) of the Vienna Convention reads:

2. The context for the purpose of the interpretation of a treaty shall comprise, in addition to the text, including its preamble and annexes:

(a) any agreement relating to the treaty which was made between all the parties in connection with the conclusion of the treaty;

(b) any instrument which was made by one or more parties in connection with the conclusion of the treaty and accepted by the other parties as an instrument related to the treaty.

3. There shall be taken into account, together with the context:

(a) any subsequent agreement between the parties regarding the interpretation of the treaty or the application of its provisions;

(b) *any subsequent practice in the application of the treaty which establishes the agreement of the parties regarding its interpretation* (emphasis added).

2 Effects of Coastline Changes on Agreed and Adjudicated Maritime Boundaries

In its 2016 Interim Report the Committee recalled that the second issue identified by the Baselines Committee was what it termed the 'negative impacts on maritime boundaries negotiated in reliance on normal baselines in existence at the time of a delimitation'.[114] In other words, two (or possibly more) States negotiate a maritime boundary delimitation agreement relying on their current baselines in order, for example, to calculate an equidistance line. Subsequently coastal baseline changes may occur as a result of inundation caused by sea level rise, leading to the loss of salient basepoints with a resultant shift in the location of baselines landward. In this scenario is it possible for one party then to argue that this is a fundamental change of circumstances which would undermine the validity of the maritime boundary agreement?

The concept of 'fundamental change of circumstances', or *clausula rebus sic stantibus*, is specifically referred to in Article 62 of the 1969 Vienna Convention on the Law of Treaties. Article 62(1) reads:

> A fundamental change of circumstances which has occurred with regard to those existing at the time of the conclusion of a treaty, and which was not foreseen by the parties, may not be invoked as a ground for terminating or withdrawing from the treaty unless:
> a) the existence of those circumstances constituted an essential basis of the consent of the parties to be bound by the treaty; and
> b) the effect of the change is radically to transform the extent of obligations still to be performed under the treaty.

However, Article 62(2) does specifically exclude two situations from the application of this doctrine. With regard to one of these situations, it provides that:

> A fundamental change of circumstances may not be invoked as a ground for terminating or withdrawing from a treaty: (a) if the treaty establishes a boundary; ...[115]

The 2016 Interim Report reviewed the literature on this provision in the Vienna Convention and noted that some scholars have suggested that its application

114 *Baselines Committee Sofia Report* (n. 3) at 423 (on-line, at 29).

115 The second exception is not relevant here: '(b) if the fundamental change is the result of a breach by the party invoking it either of an obligation under the treaty or of any other international obligation owed to any other party to the treaty'.

to maritime boundaries is still an open issue.[116] Although no express mention is made of maritime boundaries in the *travaux préparatoires*, the ILC did refer to maritime boundaries when working on a set of Articles on the Law of Treaties Between States and International Organizations or Between International Organizations. The ILC explained that the 'term "boundary" customarily denotes the limit of the land territory of a State, but it could conceivably be taken more broadly to designate the various lines which fix the spatial limits of the exercise of different powers'.[117] The ILC took the view that lines could be boundaries for certain purposes and not others, e.g., opposable to other States while not conferring exclusive jurisdiction.[118] The Commission considered that territorial sea boundaries were 'true limit[s] of the territory of the State' but that, even if other maritime boundaries, and boundaries to air space, could also be categorised as 'true boundaries', they might not fall within the boundary exclusion of Article 62(2)(a) of the Vienna Convention.[119] Therefore, the ILC had left the question open as it relates to maritime boundaries beyond those of the territorial sea.[120]

116 Those who appear to regard maritime boundaries as included within the provisions of Article 62(2), so as not to contemplate *clausula rebus sic stantibus*, include the ICJ in an *obiter dicta* in the *Aegean Sea Continental Shelf* (*Greece v. Turkey*), [1978] ICJ Reports, para. 85; Soons (n. 58), at 228; Freestone and Pethick (n. 58), at 78; C. Schofield, 'The Trouble with Islands: The Definition and Role of Islands and Rocks in Maritime Boundary Delimitation' in: Seong-Yong Hong and J. Van Dyke (n. 93) 19, 22; and, after a detailed examination of the *travaux preparatoires*, J. Lisztwan, 'Stability of Maritime Boundary Agreements' (2012) 37 *Yale Journal of International Law* 153, 186. Those who argue that the issue may be still be moot include Caron (n. 93); J. Lusthaus, 'Shifting Sands: Sea Level Rise, Maritime Boundaries and Inter-state Conflict' (2010) 30 *Politics* 113, 115–118; S. Arnadottir, 'Termination of Maritime Boundaries Due to a Fundamental Change of Circumstances' (2016) 32 *Utrecht Journal of International and European Law* 94 (which includes a discussion of arguments presented by Lisztwan); and Kaye (n. 100), at 439.

117 Yearbook of the ILC 1982, volume II, part 2 'Report of the Commission to the General Assembly on the work of the thirty-fourth session' (3 May–23 July 1982) UN Doc. A/CN.4/SER.A/1982/Add.l (Part 2) 60.

118 Ibid., 60–61.

119 Ibid., 61.

120 See further T. Giegerich, 'Article 62. Fundamental Change of Circumstances' in: O. Dörr and K. Schmalenbach (eds), *Vienna Convention on the Law of Treaties: A Commentary* (Springer, 2012) 1067, 1093. For a recent analysis of this difference regarding maritime boundaries of the territorial sea, on the one hand, and those beyond the territorial sea, on the other, and the implications for international jurisprudence see: D. Vidas, 'The Delimitation of the Territorial Sea, the Continental Shelf and the EEZ: A Comparative Perspective', in: A.G. Oude Elferink, T. Henriksen and S.V. Busch (eds), *Maritime Boundary*

The Committee also noted that in *Bangladesh v. India*, the Tribunal in its Award noted that: 'maritime delimitations, like land boundaries, must be stable and definitive to ensure a peaceful relationship between the States concerned in the long term'.[121] It went on to say that: '[i]n the view of the Tribunal, neither the prospect of climate change nor its possible effects can jeopardize the large number of settled maritime boundaries throughout the world. This applies equally to maritime boundaries agreed between States and to those established through international adjudication'.[122]

The Committee therefore took the view that although changes in coasts and baselines brought about by sea level rise or any other reason may have affected a boundary in some way, they had not to date affected the validity of an existing maritime boundary agreement.[123] Moreover, the Committee took the view that it did not need to offer a definitive view as to whether maritime boundaries were intended to be, or should be, covered by the exception to the *clausula rebus sic stantibus* rule in Article 62(2) of the Vienna Convention. But the Committee did note that the existing clear exemption of land boundaries is intended to send a strong message about the particular importance of the stability of territorial entitlements.

The Committee recalled that in section 1 of this Part of its Report it had recommended an interpretation of the 1982 LOSC which favoured preserving entitlements to maritime zones. With this in mind, it considered that the question of impacts of sea level rise on boundaries should be viewed much more widely in the context of the importance of the principles of certainty and stability of treaties, particularly those related to international borders and boundaries. Such treaties create obligations between the parties but are also relevant to third parties who might rely on them for various purposes. These principles are reflected in a range of international treaty regimes and in the jurisprudence of international courts and tribunals.

The 1982 LOSC itself stresses in its Preamble that the Convention 'will contribute to the strengthening of peace, security, cooperation and friendly relations among all nations in conformity with the principles of justice and

---

Delimitation: The Case Law. Is it Consistent and Predictable? (Cambridge University Press, 2018), 33–61.

121 *Bangladesh v. India*, Award (n. 92), para. 216.

122 Ibid., para. 217.

123 On the grounds of legal stability and certainty the Committee was sceptical as to whether this rule should be re-examined *de lege ferenda* or be subject to revision at this stage, since this could involve a revision of either or both of the LOSC and the Vienna Convention on the Law of Treaties, Article 62(2). See the *2016 Interim Report*, (n. 11), at 17.

equal rights and will promote the economic and social advancement of all peoples of the world, in accordance with the Purposes and Principles of the United Nations as set forth in the Charter'.[124]

The 1978 Vienna Convention on Succession of States in respect of Treaties recognises a special regime for boundaries.[125] It provides in Article 11 that:

> A succession of States does not as such affect:
> (a) a boundary established by a treaty; or
> (b) obligations and rights established by a treaty and relating to the regime of a boundary.

Similarly, Article 12 on 'Other territorial regimes' provides:

> 1. A succession of States does not as such affect:
> (a) obligations relating to the use of any territory, or to restrictions upon its use, established by a treaty for the benefit of any territory of a foreign State and considered as attaching to the territories in question;
> (b) rights established by a treaty for the benefit of any territory and relating to the use, or to restrictions upon the use, of any territory of a foreign State and considered as attaching to the territories in question.
> 2. A succession of States does not as such affect:
> (a) obligations relating to the use of any territory, or to restrictions upon its use, established by a treaty for the benefit of a group of States or of all States and considered as attaching to that territory;
> (b) rights established by a treaty for the benefit of a group of States or of all States and relating to the use of any territory, or to restrictions upon its use, and considered as attaching to that territory.

The Committee also noted that a large number of maritime boundaries still remained to be agreed and that the development of the modern extensive network of maritime boundary treaties has largely taken place after the finalisation of the 1969 Vienna Convention.[126] Moreover, many of the maritime

124 LOSC Preamble, para 7.

125 (1978) 72 *American Journal of International Law* 971.

126 See J.R.V. Prescott and C. Schofield, *The Maritime Political Boundaries of the World* (Brill, 2005). Also note that according to Schofield (writing in 2016) '196 of these 366 potential maritime boundaries or 54 percent of them had at least one agreement in place relating to their delimitation'; see C. Schofield, 'Seeking Lines in the Sea: Progress and Challenges in the Expansion of Maritime Claims and Delimitation of Maritime Boundaries over the

boundaries were negotiated when the phenomena of climate change and sea level rise were already becoming more widely known. The Committee, however, agreed to recommend that States negotiating future maritime boundaries pay specific attention to the possible impacts of sea level rise.

The Committee was unable to trace any situations where a party to a maritime boundary treaty had sought to set it aside for any reason. However, the Committee did examine a series of maritime boundary delimitation agreements where physical changes in coastlines or basepoints might be pertinent and grouped them loosely into three categories.

The first set of treaties – which appear to be extremely rare – relate to situations where the parties designate a method for determining the boundary line without listing detailed co-ordinates. In such a situation, changes in coastlines and basepoints would result in a change in the course of the boundary itself.[127] Two treaties negotiated by France in relation to Wallis and Futuna fall within this category. The first, concluded with Tonga in 1980, establishes an equidistance boundary to delimit the EEZs without fixing co-ordinates.[128] The second, with Tuvalu, was adopted as a provisional boundary by an exchange of notes in 1987, with a similar approach where only the method of delimitation is specified, not the co-ordinates of the boundary.[129] Here there is also an

---

Past Fifty Years', in: H.N. Scheiber, N. Oral and M-S. Kwon (eds), *Ocean Law Debates: The 50-year Legacy and Emerging Issues for the Years Ahead* (Leiden/Boston: Martinus Nijhoff, 2018).

127 In *Guyana v. Suriname*, the arbitral tribunal confirmed changes in provisional equidistance boundaries resulting from changes to relevant coastlines. When delimiting the maritime boundary the tribunal concluded that the territorial sea boundary should follow the previously agreed upon N10°E line from relevant coasts seawards to 3 nautical miles and, thereafter, intersect the equidistance line as it was at the time of delimitation. The boundary did not follow the 'historical equidistance line' beyond 3 nautical miles because it had only been fixed with an agreement up to 3 nautical miles. The new boundary followed the same methodology but resulted in a different boundary because the coastlines, on the basis of which the equidistance line was determined, had changed. *Award in the arbitration regarding the delimitation of the maritime boundary between Guyana and Suriname* (*Guyana v. Suriname*) (2007) XXX RIAA 1, para 325.

128 Convention between the Government of the French Republic (Wallis and Futuna) and the Government of the Kingdom of Tonga on the delimitation of exclusive economic zones (adopted and entered into force 11 January 1980), 1183 UNTS 343.

129 Cited by Kaye (n. 100). Exchange of Notes between France and Tuvalu Constituting an Agreement Concerning Provisional Maritime Delimitation between the Two Countries, France-Tuvalu. Aug. 6, 1985 – Nov. 5, 1985, 1506 UNTS 1987, <http://www.un.org/depts/los/LEGISLATIONANDTREATIES/PDFFILES/TREATIES/FRA-TUV1985MD.PDF>. Kaye (n. 100) reports that the text of the 2014 replacement agreement is yet to be published. See Agreement Reached Between Fiji, Tuvalu and France on Maritime Boundaries, THE COMMONWEALTH (12 December 2014), <http://thecommonwealth.org/media/news/agreement-reached-between-fiji-tuvalu-and-france-maritime-boundaries>. See also

analogy with a situation where a navigable river constitutes a land boundary and the *thalweg* – or centre of the primary navigable channel – is designated as the boundary.[130] Such a boundary may move naturally in response to physical changes.[131]

The second set of situations is where the treaty parties appear to contemplate a readjustment of a boundary once more accurate information becomes available or, as a third option, even contemplate the renegotiation of the boundary in the light of changes to baselines. Some examples of this second group include the Canada – Denmark (Greenland) Treaty of 1973, which provides in its Article III:

> In view of the inadequacies of existing hydrographic charts for certain areas and failing a precise determination of the low-water line in all sectors along the coast of Greenland and the eastern coasts of the Canadian

---

C. Redgwell, 'UNCLOS and Climate Change', (2012) 106 *American Society of International Law Proceedings* 406, 408.

130 The Oxford English Dictionary defines a thalweg as: 'A line connecting the lowest points of successive cross-sections along the course of a valley or river', <https://en.oxforddictionaries.com/definition/thalweg>. An example of the use of the thalweg is included in the 1973 Treaty between Australia and Indonesia, regarding the Fly River (see n. 133).

131 Note also recent state practice regarding 'mobile' land boundaries between Italy and Austria, and Italy and Switzerland affected by the melting of glaciers. The exchange of diplomatic notes between Italy and Switzerland of 23 and 26 May 2008 first formalises the problem of the *mobile border*, to move with the melting of the glacier. It came into force on 10 February 2010, at: <https://www.admin.ch/opc/fr/classified-compilation/20091908/index.html>. For the Italian Law of 29 May 2009 (No. 72), approving the exchanged notes into internal law, see: <http://www.normattiva.it/uri-res/N2Ls?urn:nir:stato:legge:2009-05-29;72!vig=>.

Italian Act n. 283/2005 approves into law the agreement between Italy and Austria about the new border demarcation, which dates to 1994. Law of 15 December 2005 (No. 283), available at: <http://www.normattiva.it/uri-res/N2Ls?urn:nir:stato:legge:2005-12-15;283!vig=>. Article 3(2) of the agreement concerns the mobile border and states: 'Where the State border is defined by the watershed or ridge line, it follows the gradual natural alterations to which such lines are subject. By contrast, sudden natural alterations or manmade alterations to the watershed or ridge line do not entail any change to the path of the border'. Natural alteration includes melting of the glacier: like the examples regarding rivers (see below), this State practice is not directly related to maritime boundaries, but it is closely related to the overall cause of sea level rise (climate change) and partly also to one of the direct contributors of rising sea levels, i.e., to glacier melting. Thanks to Andrea Bagnato and Marco Ferrari of the *Italian Limes Project* (see at: <http://www.italianlimes.net/> last accessed 8 June 2018) for supplying the Committee Chair with relevant information about this novel State practice between Italy and Austria and Switzerland, respectively, and for assisting with translation of the documents.

> Arctic Islands, neither Party shall issue licences ... in areas bordering the dividing line without the prior agreement of the other Party ...

It then goes on to provide in Article IV (2):

> If new surveys or resulting charts or maps should indicate that the dividing line requires adjustment, the Parties agree that an adjustment will be carried out on the basis of the same principle as those used in determining the dividing line, and such adjustment shall be provided for in a Protocol to this Agreement.[132]

Another example is the 1973 Agreements between Australia and Indonesia Concerning Certain Boundaries between Papua New Guinea and Indonesia. In accordance with its Article 1(b), the second section of the agreed boundary follows 'the waterway ("thalweg") of the Fly River (at present located at Latitude 6° 19' 24" South.)'. Because of the instability of the coast at the terminus of the land boundary and the start of the maritime boundary, Article 2 of the Agreement contemplates that the parties 'shall arrange for aerial or satellite photography of that part of the Fly River referred to in Article 1(b) of this Agreement. Thereafter, such photography of that part of the Fly River shall be arranged periodically at intervals to be agreed upon'. In Article 9 the Agreement includes the proviso that the 'actual location' of the coordinates mentioned will be determined by the 'competent authorities' of the parties concerned.[133]

The 2003 State Border Regime Treaty between Romania and Ukraine also provides that 'objective modifications due to natural phenomena' may lead to the revision of coordinates.[134]

---

132 J.I. Charney and L.M. Alexander (eds), *International Maritime Boundaries* (Springer: Netherlands, 1993) Vol. I, at 384. Thanks to Captain Ash Roach for drawing this and other such treaties to our attention.

133 Agreement between Australia and Indonesia Concerning Certain Boundaries between Papua New Guinea and Indonesia, signed 12 February 1973, entered into force 26 November 1974, 975 UNTS 3. Thanks to Clive Schofield for identifying this example.

134 Article 1 of the Treaty between Romania and Ukraine on the Romanian – Ukrainian State border regime, collaboration and mutual assistance on border matters, entered into force 27 May 2004, 2277 UNTS 3. Thanks to Snjólaug Árnadóttir for bringing this to our attention. Note also that the ICJ decided not to establish a fixed boundary for the first 3 nautical miles of the maritime boundary between Nicaragua and Honduras, leaving it up to the States to determine and adjust that segment with consideration for the changing coastline. *Territorial and Maritime Dispute between Nicaragua and Honduras in the Caribbean Sea (Nicaragua v. Honduras)* (Judgment) [2007] ICJ Reports, para 311.

In the third group of boundary agreements – contemplating renegotiation in the light of changes to baselines – is the 1990 Treaty between the Cook Islands and France (French Polynesia). Article 3 provides:

> If new surveys or resulting charts and maps should indicate that changes in the base points co-ordinates are sufficiently significant to require adjustments of the maritime boundary, the Parties agree that an adjustment will be carried out on the basis of the same principles as those used in determining the maritime boundary, and such adjustments shall be provided for in a Protocol to this Agreement.[135]

In all these situations, the parties explicitly contemplate that more information is needed or that physical changes might occur. Consequently, it is difficult for them to argue that a physical change in a baseline constitutes a fundamental change of circumstances 'not foreseen by the parties'.[136] It has also been pointed out that the Vienna Convention sets an 'exceptionally high burden' for allowing the existence of a fundamental change of circumstances.[137] To dispute the validity of a maritime boundary treaty (if indeed Article 62(2) of the Vienna Convention may be interpreted to contemplate this),[138] it would need to be shown that the position of the established coastal basepoints at the time of the conclusion of the agreement amounted to a circumstance that 'constituted an essential basis of the consent of the parties to be bound by treaty' and that the effect of sea level rise 'is *radically* to transform the extent of obligations still to be performed under the treaty'.[139]

---

135 *International Maritime Boundaries*, Charney and Alexander (n. 132), at 1181.

136 Other examples include: Australia-Indonesia (seabed boundaries), 1971, Article 6(1), II IMB 1204; Australia – Indonesia (Timor and Arafura Seas), 1972, Article 6, II IMB 1217; India – Indonesia, 1977, Article 3(2), II IMB 1377; Burma – Thailand, 1980, Article 2(2), II IMB 1351; India – Indonesia, 1974, Article 1(3), II IMB 1369; India – Indonesia – Thailand, 1978, Article 1(6), II IMB 1387; India – Maldives, 1976, Article III, II IMB 1398; India – Maldives – Sri Lanka, 1976, Article III, II IMB 1408; India – Sri Lanka (historic waters), 1974, Article 3, II IMB 1416–17; India – Thailand, 1978, Article 2(2), II IMB 1441; Malaysia – Thailand (territorial sea), 1979, Article III, I IMB 1997; Indonesia – Thailand (Malacca), 1971, Article 1(4), II IMB 1462–63 ('at the request of either Government'). With thanks to Captain Ashley Roach for these examples.

137 Kaye (n. 100), at 439.

138 See discussion above, and the literature referred to in n. 116 and n. 120.

139 Vienna Convention, Article 62(1)(a) and(b); emphasis added.

2.1 *Proposal of the Committee*

As indicated above, the Committee took the view that it did not need to come to a determination as to whether it considered Article 62(2) of the 1969 Vienna Convention to apply to maritime boundaries. In its 2016 Interim Report, the Committee had expressed its preliminary view in favour of a presumption of certainty and stability of all boundary treaties.[140] Such a presumption would argue against the use of the *rebus sic stantibus* doctrine to upset maritime boundary treaties on the ground of physical changes arising from sea level rise. The Committee was unaware of any situations where such an argument had been put forward and knew of none where it had been substantiated. Although it was acutely conscious of the potential for major physical impacts on coastal geography that sea level rise could have in a relatively longer-term perspective, the Committee felt that the interests of the international community would at this stage not be best served by a proposal undermining existing negotiated and established maritime boundaries. It also noted that if its recommendations regarding the maintenance of existing entitlements to maritime zones were accepted, then the same principle should apply to maritime areas delimited by international agreements. Indeed, the same approach should also be taken in cases of maritime boundaries established by judgments of international courts or by arbitral awards.

The Committee therefore recommended a proposal to this effect to be put together in a Resolution of the International Law Association. The Committee proposed that, on the grounds of legal certainty and stability, the impacts of sea level rise on maritime boundaries, whether contemplated or not by the parties at the time of the negotiation of the maritime boundary, should not be regarded as a fundamental change of circumstances. The Committee further recommended that the interpretation of the 1982 Law of the Sea Convention which it proposed in relation to the ability of coastal States to maintain their existing lawful maritime entitlements should apply equally to maritime areas delimited by international agreement or by decisions of international courts or arbitral tribunals.

B *Issues of Statehood and International Legal Personality in the Case of Total Loss of State Territory or Its Becoming Permanently Uninhabitable*

The Committee discussed a range of issues posed by the inundation of islands and territories by sea level rise, including whether any maintenance of a coastal State's maritime zones should continue once the viable population of

140 *2016 Interim Report* (n. 11), at 17.

a coastal or archipelagic State has moved or is resettled due to sea level rise, and what would be the effects of submergence of the entire territory of a State on its maritime zones? Could, for instance, historic rights be considered as the legal basis for the maintenance of maritime zones within previously defined limits and boundaries of a State whose territory is affected by submergence due to sea level rise? If so, to what subject of international law would such historic rights belong? Moreover, and relatedly: would the impact of sea level rise require the creation of a new category of subjects of international law? What could be the role of an agreement between a State affected by submergence of its territory and a host State (implying both international and constitutional law aspects) regarding the possibility of performance of rights that are at present normally attributed to coastal States based on their territory?

Committee members took the view that the international law rules on the acquisition and loss of territory were clear and well established[141] and that there had been numerous situations in the past where governments have existed without physical control of territory – as for example in the cases of governments in exile. The Committee was, however, conscious of the fact that there have been no precedents for the situation which might initially be faced by a small number of island States if sea level rise reached existential proportions for them. It was also stressed that the future challenges of sea level rise are of a profoundly novel and different nature, caused by changes of unprecedented proportions and driven by natural forces rather than by political circumstances.

While it was generally agreed that, as guidance and as a starting point, there should be a presumption of continuing statehood in cases where land territory was lost, the Committee felt that the exact modalities for the continuation of statehood, or perhaps some other form of international legal personality, as well as other solutions for this problem (e.g., merger with another State), were questions of great sensitivity that the Committee should approach with considerable caution. The attention of the Committee was also drawn to the political dimensions of the issues involved.

The Committee therefore agreed not to continue its discussions on this issue at this point and considered that it would be useful to extend the Committee's term beyond 2018, in order to enable a closer focus on these fundamental issues as well as other related matters, including, especially, transitional issues and how to deal with diminishing statehood as a process.

---

141 International law traditionally recognises five methods of acquisition of title to territory: occupation; prescription; conquest; cession; accretion and avulsion; see further R.Y. Jennings, *The Acquisition of Territory in International Law* (Manchester University Press, 1963).

Part III: Sydney Declaration of Principles on the Protection of Persons Displaced in the Context of Sea Level Rise

In accordance with its mandate to study the 'implications under international law of the partial and complete inundation of state territory, or depopulation thereof, in particular of small island and low-lying states', the Committee decided to focus on the protection of persons displaced in the context of sea level rise as one of its priority areas. Its Interim Report submitted to the Johannesburg Conference (2016) addressed in Part III issues relating to human rights and mobility.[142] It identified a series of 'tools' required to address the implications of sea level rise on humans both in terms of interventions that would enable affected persons to remain *in situ*, as well as those that would assist them to move either within their own country or to another country. The notion of 'human mobility'[143] is used as an umbrella term that refers to all relevant forms of the movement of persons and, in the context of this report, covers displacement (which is forced), migration (which is predominantly voluntary), planned relocation (which may be forced or voluntary), and evacuations (which may be forced or voluntary).

Building on the Interim Report, the Committee discussed during its intersessional meetings in Lopud, Croatia (September 2017) and Singapore (March 2018) a series of principles that codify and progressively develop relevant norms of international law. This part of the report of the Committee takes the form of draft principles entitled the 'Sydney Declaration of Principles on the Protection of Persons Displaced in the Context of Sea Level Rise' with commentaries.

---

142 See the *2016 Interim Report* (n. 11). For a more detailed analysis, see J. McAdam, B. Burson, W. Kälin and S. Weerasinghe, *International Law and Sea-Level Rise: Forced Migration and Human Rights* (FNI Report 1/2016), available at <https://www.fni.no/publications/international-law-and-sea-level-rise-forced-migration-and-human-rights-article893-290.html> accessed 8 June 2018.

143 There is no internationally agreed definition of human mobility, but the notion is increasingly used as an umbrella term covering different forms of such mobility, including in the New York Declaration for Refugees and Migrants, UNGA res 71/1 of 19 September 2016 (3 October 2016) para 3; 'Sendai Framework for Disaster Risk Reduction 2015–2030' UNGA res 69/283 (23 June 2015) para 30(l) (Sendai Framework); and UNFCCC Conference of the Parties, Decision 3/CP.18, Approaches to address loss and damage associated with climate change impacts in developing countries that are particularly vulnerable to the adverse effects of climate change to enhance adaptive capacity, in *Report of the Conference of the Parties on its eighteenth session, held in Doha from 26 November to 8 December 2012: Addendum: Part Two: Action taken by the Conference of the Parties at its eighteenth session*, UN Doc. FCCC/CP/2012/8/Add.1, 22–23, para 7(a)(vi).

SYDNEY DECLARATION OF PRINCIPLES ON THE PROTECTION OF PERSONS DISPLACED IN THE CONTEXT OF SEA LEVEL RISE

Purpose

The purpose of the present Declaration of Principles is to provide guidance to States in averting, mitigating, and addressing displacement of persons occurring in the context of sea level rise, based on and derived from relevant international legal provisions, principles, and frameworks.

Commentary

The movement of persons away from fragile and unstable coastal areas is already a reality. With continuing sea level rise, large numbers of persons are expected to move away from low-lying coastal zones and atoll islands in the coming decades.[144] Persons displaced across borders in the context of sea level rise are not recognised as refugees unless, in an individual case, elements of persecution are present. Current legal instruments do not explicitly address the movement of persons across borders in anticipation of future climate change-related harm. Despite these gaps in international law, States affected by rising sea levels, as well as transit and destination States faced with this phenomenon in cases of cross-border movement, need guidance, particularly if such movements are large-scale.[145] Such guidance can be derived from international human rights law as well as other relevant international legal principles and frameworks, including in the areas of international cooperation, disaster risk management and reduction, and climate change.

Scope

The present Declaration of Principles applies to all forms of human mobility arising in the context of sea level rise.

---

144 See, e.g., IPCC, *Summary for Policymakers*, in: *Climate Change 2014: Impacts, Adaptation, and Vulnerability, Part A: Global and Sectoral Aspects, Contribution of Working Group II to the Fifth Assessment Report of the Intergovernmental Panel on Climate Change* (Cambridge University Press, 2014), 20; W. Adger et al., 'Human Security', in: *Climate Change 2014: Impacts, Adaptation, and Vulnerability, Part A: Global and Sectoral Aspects. Contribution of Working Group II to the Fifth Assessment Report of the Intergovernmental Panel on Climate Change* (Cambridge University Press, 2014), 775; K. Rigaud et al., *Groundswell: Preparing for Internal Climate Migration* (World Bank, 2018).

145 See Institut du Droit International, Session de Hyderabad, 16th Committee, 'Mass Migration', Final Resolution (9 September 2017).

Commentary

Human mobility in the context of sea level rise takes several forms, including displacement (e.g. by coastal flooding or storm surges), rapid and temporary evacuations away from hazards, voluntary migration as a longer-term coping strategy, and permanent planned relocation when areas of origin are no longer habitable. In order to prevent or mitigate displacement, effective approaches to the challenges of sea level rise must address all forms of human mobility.

Mobility in the context of climate change and disasters is a multi-causal phenomenon. The effects of those triggers interact with other economic, social, and political drivers (or stressors), which themselves affect displacement and migration.[146] Furthermore, displacement, migration, and other forms of movement may be triggered by both the slow-onset consequences of sea level rise, such as coastal erosion, or by sudden-onset disasters. In some cases, it can even be triggered by a combination of both slow-onset and sudden-onset consequences. For instance, sea level rise may exacerbate storm surges, leading to salt-water intrusion into surface water and corruption of the fresh water lens.

Definitions

For the purposes of the present Declaration of Principles, the following definitions shall apply:

(*a*) *'disaster' means a serious disruption of the functioning of a community or a society at any scale, due to climatic events interacting with conditions of exposure, vulnerability, and capacity, leading to human, material, economic, and/or environmental losses and impacts;*

(*b*) *'displacement' means the movement within a State and/or across international borders of persons who are forced or obliged to leave their homes or places of habitual residence due to sudden-onset natural hazards and/or slower, cumulative pressures occurring in the context of sea level rise;*

(*c*) *'evacuation' means the rapid movement of persons away from the immediate threat or impact of a disaster to a place of shelter, in order to ensure their security, safety, and well-being;*

146 See, e.g., Foresight, *Migration and Global Environmental Change: Future Challenges and Opportunities: Final Project Report* (Government Office for Science 2011) <https://sustainabledevelopment.un.org/content/documents/867migrationscience.pdf> accessed 8 June 2018; J. McAdam, *Climate Change, Forced Migration, and International Law* (Oxford University Press, 2012), especially chapter 1, synthesising other research.

(*d*) *'human mobility' means all relevant forms of the movement of persons in the context of sea level rise, including displacement, evacuation, migration, and planned relocation;*

(*e*) *'migration' means predominantly voluntary cross-border movement, which, in the context of disaster- and climate change-related impacts, is more likely to occur in anticipation of future harm;*

(*f*) *'planned relocation' means a planned process in which persons voluntarily move or are forced to move away from their homes or places of temporary residence, are settled in a new location within their own or another State, and are provided with the conditions for rebuilding their lives. Planned relocation is carried out under the authority of the State, and is undertaken to protect persons from risks and impacts related to disasters and environmental change in the context of sea level rise;*

(*g*) *'sea level rise' means the sole or combined and cumulative impacts of the effects of climate change and subsidence or land uplift on the change of the sea level in a given location.*

Commentary

These definitions of disaster,[147] displacement,[148] evacuation,[149] human mobility,[150] migration,[151] and planned relocation[152] reproduce or build on

147 See UNISDR terminology at <http://www.unisdr.org/we/inform/terminology#letter-d> accessed 8 June 2018.

148 Adapted from UN Economic and Social Council, Commission on Human Rights, *Report of the Representative of the Secretary-General, Mr. Francis M. Deng, submitted pursuant to Commission Resolution 1997/39: Addendum, Guiding Principles on Internal Displacement*, UN Doc. E/CN.4/1998/53/Add.2 (11 February 1998) Introductory Note, para 2.

149 Adapted from Camp Coordination and Camp Management Cluster, 'The MEND Guide: Comprehensive Guide for Planning Mass Evacuations in Natural Disasters: Pilot Document', 16–17. <http://www.globalcccmcluster.org/tools-and-guidance/publications/mend-guide> accessed 8 June 2018.

150 See above, n. 143.

151 See The Nansen Initiative, *Agenda for the Protection of Cross-Border Displaced Persons in the Context of Disasters and Climate Change* (Vol. 1, December 2015) <https://nanseninitiative.org/wp-content/uploads/2015/02/PROTECTION-AGENDA-VOLUME-1.pdf> accessed 8 June 2018, para 20.

152 Adapted from Brookings/Georgetown University/UNHCR, 'Guidance on Protecting People from Disasters and Environmental Change through Planned Relocation' (7 October 2015) <https://www.brookings.edu/wp-content/uploads/2016/06/GUIDANCE_PLANNED-RELOCATION_14-OCT-2015.pdf> accessed 8 June 2018, 9 (Guidance on Planned Relocation).

definitions developed by different UN bodies and other relevant organisations and processes.

The definition of disaster used here is based on concepts developed in the area of disaster management.[153] It highlights the fact that climate-related hazards only lead to disasters if people are exposed to them and lack the resilience to withstand and cope with their impacts. It therefore highlights the multi-causality of human mobility in the context of sea level rise better than the definition adopted by the ILC which was developed for a broader purpose.[154]

Further to the content of the definitions above, it should be noted that evacuations are usually short-term (hours to weeks) and may be voluntary or forced. They usually take place within the same State rather than across an international border. Migration is usually planned, less sudden than displacement, and occurs over a longer period of time. A planned relocation can be either forced or voluntary, large-scale or small-scale, internal or cross-border.

While there is no universally accepted definition of sea level rise, the definition used for the purposes of this declaration highlights that sea levels are influenced not only by increase of the masses of water due to glacier melting and their expansion due to warmer temperatures but may also be determined by geological factors such as subsidence or land uplift that may or may not be linked to climate change.[155] This aspect of sea level rise, rather than global increases, is relevant since impacts of rising sea level that trigger the movement of people are always local.

Principle 1 – The Primary Duty and Responsibility of States to Protect and Assist Affected Persons

States have the primary duty and responsibility to provide protection and assistance to persons with habitual residence in territories under their jurisdiction who are affected by sea level rise.

Commentary

This primary duty and responsibility of States to protect and assist persons affected by sea level rise reflects the principle of sovereignty as enshrined

153 See above, n. 147.

154 Draft Articles on the Protection of Persons in the Event of Disasters, adopted by the International Law Commission (ILC) at its 68th session in 2016 and submitted to the General Assembly as part of the ILC's report of that session: UN General Assembly Official Records Supp No 10, UN Doc. A/71/10, Article 3(a).

155 See, e.g., A. Rovere, P. Stocchi and M. Vacchi, 'Eustatic and Relative Sea Level Changes' (2016) 2 *Current Climate Change Reports* 221.

in Principle 2(7) of the UN Charter. With regard to internally displaced persons, the primary responsibility of States to provide them with protection and humanitarian assistance is recognised by the 1998 UN Guiding Principles on Internal Displacement.[156] More generally, the same principle is enshrined in the ILC Draft Articles on the Protection of Persons in the Event of Disasters[157] and several General Assembly Resolutions on humanitarian assistance with regard to all persons affected by a disaster.[158] The primary duty and responsibility of States to protect persons affected by sea level rise also derives from their obligations under international human rights law and principles (see Principle 2 below). The 'primary' responsibility of States is complemented by the responsibility of the international community to cooperate with States affected by sea level rise (see Principle 4 below).

Principle 2 – The Duty to Respect the Human Rights of Affected Persons

States of origin, transit, and destination have a duty to respect, on a non-discriminatory basis, the human rights of persons under their jurisdiction who move in the context of sea level rise, including:

(*a*) *their right to liberty of movement and freedom to choose their residence;*
(*b*) *the freedom to leave and return to their own country;*
(*c*) *their right to be protected against* refoulement*;*
(*d*) *their right to be informed and consulted, and to participate in decisions affecting them;*
(*e*) *the cultural and land rights of indigenous peoples and local communities.*

Commentary

Human rights law sets out minimum standards of treatment that States must afford to all individuals within their territory and/or subject to their jurisdiction. Whether expressed as civil and political rights, or as economic, social, or

156 Guiding Principles on Internal Displacement (n. 148) principle 3; 'Strengthening of the coordination of emergency humanitarian assistance of the United Nations', UNGA res 71/127 (24 January 2017) preambular para 22.

157 Draft Articles on the Protection of Persons in the Event of Disasters (n. 154), Article 10.

158 See, e.g., 'Humanitarian assistance to victims of natural disasters and similar emergency situations' UNGA res 45/100 (14 December 1990) preambular para 3; 'Strengthening of the coordination of humanitarian emergency assistance of the United Nations', UNGA res 46/182 (19 December 1991) annex, principle 4.

cultural rights, they are underpinned by the fundamental notion that they are derived from the inherent dignity of every human being without distinction. The duty to respect human rights, which is characterised as a negative obligation, requires States to refrain from violating or otherwise interfering with the enjoyment of guaranteed human rights. The duties to protect and to fulfil human rights are characterised as positive obligations (see Principle 3).

Under existing international and regional human rights law,[159] States have duties to respect, protect, and fulfil human rights so as to protect persons from foreseeable harms emanating from the impacts of climate change, including sea level rise.[160] Any policies and strategies addressing human mobility must therefore be developed and executed in a manner fully consistent with the minimum standards of protection articulated under human rights law in a range of international and regional instruments and principles.

Principle 2 highlights just some of the rights that experience indicates are particularly relevant for persons moving in the context of sea level rise. However, its impacts will affect many other rights as well, including the rights to private and family life, property and housing, means of subsistence, freedom of residence, freedom of movement, the right not to be subjected to serious risks to life or to cruel, inhuman, or degrading treatment, and the right to freely dispose of natural resources. Moreover, impacts of sea level rise are likely to acutely and disproportionately affect vulnerable groups, including indigenous populations, women, children, the elderly, persons with disabilities, and the poor.[161]

---

159 See, in particular, International Covenant on Civil and Political Rights (adopted 16 December 1966, entered into force 23 March 1976) 999 UNTS 171 (ICCPR); International Covenant on Economic, Social and Cultural Rights (adopted 16 December 1966, entered into force 3 January 1976) 993 UNTS 3 (ICESCR); American Convention on Human Rights 'Pact of San José, Costa Rica' (adopted 22 November 1969, entered into force 18 July 1978) 1144 UNTS 143 (American Convention); African Charter on Human and Peoples' Rights (adopted 27 June 1981, entered into force 21 October 1986) (1982) 21 ILM 58 (African Charter); Convention for the Protection of Human Rights and Fundamental Freedoms, Rome, 4 November 1950, as amended by Protocols Nos 11 and 14, supplemented by Protocols Nos 1, 4, 6, 7, 12, and 13 (European Convention on Human Rights).

160 For a comprehensive overview on human rights obligations relating to climate change, see Human Rights Council, *Report of the Special Rapporteur on the Issue of Human Rights Obligations relating to the Enjoyment of a Safe, Clean, Healthy and Sustainable Environment*, UN Doc. A/HRC/31/52 (1 February 2016) paras 33–84.

161 For detailed analysis, see McAdam, Burson, Kälin and Weerasinghe (n. 142), paras 24–45; Office of the High Commissioner for Human Rights, *Report of the Office of the United Nations High Commissioner for Human Rights on the Relationship between Climate Change and Human Rights*, UN Doc. A/HRC/10/61 (15 January 2009).

Principle 3 – The Duty to Take Positive Action

1. *States have a duty to use the best practicable means at their disposal, in accordance with their respective capabilities and resources and their international human rights obligations, as well as other relevant international standards and frameworks, to take appropriate and effective measures, including those referred to in Principles 5–9, to:*
   (*a*) *reduce disaster risks and adapt to the adverse effects of climate change in order to protect the lives and ensure the safety of persons with habitual residence on low-lying areas at risk of sea level rise under their jurisdiction;*
   (*b*) *prevent displacement of such persons; and*
   (*c*) *protect and assist them in the event of displacement.*
2. *In order to avert, mitigate, and address displacement in the context of sea level rise, and to protect and assist persons displaced in this context, States should, in particular:*
   (*a*) *adopt adequate normative frameworks and operational measures to implement them;*
   (*b*) *assign powers and responsibilities to competent authorities and institutions or, where they do not exist, create such authorities and institutions endowed with appropriate powers and responsibilities; and*
   (*c*) *provide adequate resources to such authorities and institutions.*

Commentary

The duty to take positive action to protect persons against foreseeable natural hazards, as well as to respond where persons have already been affected, derives first and foremost from international human rights law and principles. Emerging jurisprudence from the European Court of Human Rights and UN treaty bodies has shed light on the ways in which States' obligations not only to respect but also to protect and fulfil certain human rights relate to phases of disaster response.[162] Arguments have also been made that victims of natural disasters can claim a right to humanitarian assistance when in need, pursuant to existing human rights.[163]

---

162 W. Kälin, 'The Human Rights Dimension of Natural or Human-Made Disasters' (2012) 55 *German Yearbook of International Law* 119, 128–29; S. McInerney-Lankford, M. Darrow and L. Rajamani, *Human Rights and Climate Change: A Review of the International Legal Dimensions* (The World Bank Group 2011).

163 Kälin (n. 162) 141.

The International Covenant on Civil and Political Rights (ICCPR), as well as regional human rights conventions, explicitly oblige States to 'protect the right to life'.[164] Article 4 of the ICCPR provides that this right is non-derogable, even in times of a 'public emergency which threatens the life of the nation'. The UN Human Rights Committee has recognised that this may include a 'natural catastrophe'.[165] As the European Court on Human Rights has highlighted, this duty to protect also applies to situations where a natural hazard is imminent and clearly identifiable, and especially 'where it concern[s] a recurring calamity affecting a distinct area developed for human habitation or use'.[166]

Paragraph 2 above lists, in a non-exhaustive manner, measures that are indispensable for States to avert, mitigate and address displacement in the context of sea level rise and to protect and assist those displaced in this context. To the extent that the effects of sea level rise are life-threatening, the positive obligation on States to take appropriate steps to safeguard the lives of those under their jurisdiction 'entails above all a primary duty on the State to put in place a legislative and administrative framework designed to provide effective deterrence against threats to the right to life'.[167] Besides the duty to take *preventative action* (to avert potential violations), the duty to protect also entails obligations with regard to *remedial action* (to address the consequences of a violation), and requires operational, legislative, and/or enforcement measures to be put in place.[168] In this regard 'an impossible or disproportionate burden must not be imposed on the authorities', and States retain some margin of appreciation, dependent in part on the resources at their disposal, with regard to operational choices.[169]

Beyond protecting the right to life, the existence of a positive obligation on States to take steps to protect against the socio-economic impacts of disasters, including those arising from sea level rise, has been emphasised by the UN

---

164 ICCPR, Article 6; American Convention, Article 4; African Charter, Article 4; European Convention on Human Rights, Article 2.

165 UN Human Rights Committee General Comment No 29 (2001) 'Article 4: Derogations during a state of emergency', UN Doc. CCPR/C/21/Rev.1/Add.11 (31 August 2001) para 5.

166 *Budayeva and Others v Russia*, App Nos 15339/02, 21166/02, 20058/02, 11673/02 and 15343/02, ECHR 2008-II, para 137.

167 Ibid., paras 128–29.

168 See W. Kälin and J. Künzli, *The Law of International Human Rights Protection* (Oxford University Press, 2009) 96, 106–07. Treaty monitoring bodies recognise that even human rights guarantees containing no explicit reference to a duty to protect may nevertheless entail such an obligation.

169 *Budayeva* (n. 166) paras 134–35. Similarly, see the New Zealand jurisprudence, e.g., *AC (Tuvalu)* [2014] NZIPT 800517–520, para 75.

Committee on Economic, Social and Cultural Rights.[170] The rights of specific groups that may be more vulnerable to the impacts of sea level rise are also being increasingly recognised. For instance, Article 11 of the Convention on the Rights of Persons with Disabilities explicitly obliges States to take 'all necessary measures to ensure the protection and safety of persons with disabilities in situations of risk, including … the occurrence of natural disasters'.[171]

Principle 4 – The Duty to Cooperate

1. *States shall enhance international cooperation among themselves and with relevant international organisations and agencies to assist States affected by sea level rise to prevent, avoid, and respond to disaster- and climate change-related risks, including the risk of displacement. Affected States should call on the international community when they require assistance.*
2. *Cooperation in this context may include:*
   (*a*) *efforts at bilateral, regional and/or sub-regional levels to strengthen and coordinate measures to:*
      i. reduce disaster-risk, enhance adaptation to climate change, and build resilience of affected communities living in low-lying areas at risk of sea level rise;
      ii. assist, in accordance with elementary humanitarian considerations, in the evacuation of persons where necessary to save lives, including across borders;

170 UN Committee on Economic, Social and Cultural Rights (CESCR) General Comment No. 7 (1997) 'The Right to Adequate Housing, Article 11, paragraph 1, of the Covenant: Forced evictions' in Committee on Economic, Social and Cultural Rights, *Report on the Sixteenth and Seventeenth Sessions (28 April–16 May 1997, 17 November–5 December 1997)*, Economic and Social Council Official Records, 1998, Supp No. 2 (E/1998/22) annex IV, paras 8(b), 8(d), 8(e); CESCR 'General Comment 12: The Right to Adequate Food (Art. 11)', UN Doc. E/C.12/1999/5 (12 May 1999) para 13; CESCR General Comment No. 15 (2002) 'The right to water (arts 11 and 12 of the International Covenant on Economic, Social and Cultural Rights)', UN Doc. E/C.12/2002/11 (20 January 2003) para 16(h).

171 Convention on the Rights of Persons with Disabilities (adopted 13 December 2006, entered into force 3 May 2008) 2515 UNTS 3, Article 11. The UN Committee on the Rights of Persons with Disabilities regularly urges States to integrate persons with disabilities explicitly into disaster management and disaster risk reduction strategies. See, e.g., UN Committee on the Rights of Persons with Disabilities (CRPD), 'Concluding Observations on the Initial Report of the Czech Republic', UN Doc. CRPD/C/CZE/CO/1 (15 May 2015) para 21; CRPD, 'Concluding Observations on the Initial Report of Mauritius', UN Doc. CRPD/C/MUS/CO/1 (30 September 2015) para 20; CRPD, 'Concluding Observations on the Initial Report of Qatar', UN Doc. CRPD/C/QAT/CO/1 (2 October 2015) Article 11.

iii. *facilitate cross-border migration in anticipation of, or in reaction to, irreversible environmental degradation or sudden-onset disasters linked to sea level rise;*
iv. *enhance the humanitarian response in situations of internal displacement; and*
v. *support recovery, including durable solutions, for internally displaced persons;*

(*b*) *efforts to ensure that persons moving across borders are admitted and received with respect for their safety, dignity, and human rights, including the creation or harmonisation of more predictable domestic or regional legal frameworks, and that durable solutions to displacement are found; and*

(*c*) *technical and financial support by the international community and donor States and their multilateral and bilateral financing mechanisms to support affected States and regions.*

Commentary

The duty to cooperate is a fundamental principle of international law. It is a core objective of the UN Charter,[172] reflected in many other international instruments,[173] and is considered key to achieving international peace and

172 Article 1(3) of the UN Charter lists one of the four purposes of the UN as being: 'To achieve international cooperation in solving international problems of an economic, social, cultural, or humanitarian character, and in promoting and encouraging respect for human rights and for fundamental freedoms for all without distinction as to race, sex, language, or religion'. Article 56 provides: 'All Members pledge themselves to take joint and separate action in cooperation with the Organization for the achievement of the purposes set forth in Article 55'. See Charter of the United Nations (adopted 26 June 1945, entered into force 24 October 1945) (UN Charter).

173 See, e.g., ICESCR, Arts 2(1), 11, 15, 22, 23; 'Declaration on Principles of International Law concerning Friendly Relations and Co-operation among States in accordance with the Charter of the United Nations', UNGA res 2625 (XXV) (24 October 1970) annex, para 1; Rio Declaration on Environment and Development, in *Report of the United Nations Conference on Environment and Development* (Rio de Janeiro, 3–14 June 1992) (Vol I) A/CONF.151/26/Rev.1 (1993) annex I, principles 5, 7, 13, 24, 27; United Nations Framework Convention on Climate Change (adopted 9 May 1992, entered into force 21 March 1994) 1771 UNTS 107 (UNFCCC) Arts 4(1)(c), (d), (e), (g), (h), (i), 5(c), 6(b); Draft Articles on the Prevention of Transboundary Harm from Hazardous Activities, adopted by the ILC at its 53rd session in 2001 and submitted to the General Assembly as part of the ILC's report of that session: UN General Assembly Official Records, Supp 10, UN Doc. A/56/10, Arts 4, 14, 16; Declaration of the United Nations Conference on the Human Environment (adopted 16 June 1972) (Stockholm Declaration) in *Report of the United Nations Conference on the Human Environment: Stockholm, 5–16 June 1972*, UN Doc. A/CONF.48/14/Rev.1, principles 22, 24; see also CESCR General Comment No. 2 (1990) 'International technical

security. It generally refers to two or more States working together towards a common goal.

The challenges presented by the adverse impacts of sea level rise may make it difficult for some States to discharge their human rights obligations on their own. This is likely to worsen over time. While sea level rise is a challenge for all States, it is poorer States that will be disproportionately affected, with their responsive capacity already hampered by insufficient resources, limited technical and institutional support, and other stressors such as population growth, few educational opportunities, and weak human rights protection. Significantly, it is those Small Island Developing States (SIDS) facing the greatest threats from the impacts of sea level rise which may possess the least domestic responsive capacity, and are thus the greatest potential beneficiaries of enhanced international cooperation. Such States will require support – technical, financial, and operational – to assist and protect their own populations and to respect, protect, and fulfil their human rights obligations. In particular, the International Covenant on Economic, Social and Cultural Rights, Article 2(1) obliges each State party 'to take steps, individually and through international assistance and co-operation, especially economic and technical, to the maximum of its available resources, with a view to achieving progressively the full realization of the rights recognized in the present Covenant by all appropriate means'. While acknowledging a wide margin of appreciation in this regard, this not only entails, at least in principle, the duty of States affected by sea level rise to turn to the international community for support, but arguably also entails at least a general obligation of other States to provide needed support either bilaterally or collectively through the UN humanitarian and development agencies, the

assistance measures (Article 22 of the Covenant)', in Committee on Economic, Social and Cultural Rights, *Report on the Fourth Session (15 January–2 February 1990)*, Economic and Social Council Official Records, 1990, Supp No. 3 (E/1990/23) annex III; CESCR General Comment No. 3 (1990) 'The nature of States parties obligations (Art. 2, para 1 of the Covenant)', in Committee on Economic, Social and Cultural Rights, *Report on the Fifth Session (26 November–14 December 1990)*, Economic and Social Council Official Records, 1991, Supp No. 3 (E/1991/23) annex III; CESCR General Comment No. 7 (n. 170); CESCR General Comment No. 14 (2000) 'The right to the highest attainable standard of health (Article 12 of the International Covenant on Economic, Social and Cultural Rights)', UN Doc. E/C.12/2000/4 (11 August 2000); CESCR General Comment No. 15 (n. 170). The Disabilities Convention states that the right to cooperate applies 'in situations of risk, including situations of armed conflict, humanitarian emergencies and the occurrence of natural disasters': Convention on the Rights of Persons with Disabilities, Article 11. In the context of natural disasters specifically, see UNGA res 46/182 (n. 171) annex, principle 5; Draft Articles on the Protection of Persons in the event of Disasters (n. 157) Article 5; Guiding Principles on Internal Displacement (n. 148) principle 3.

funding mechanisms for humanitarian action, the development banks, and the 'Green Climate Fund'[174] supporting States to adapt to the effects of climate change.

These aspects are an expression of the principle of common but differentiated responsibilities[175] as envisioned by the UN Framework Convention on Climate Change (UNFCCC) and associated instruments which are based on the need for the international community to take collective responsibility for a problem of its own making.[176] Other instruments that are relevant include: (i) paragraph 14(f) of the Cancún Adaptation Framework,[177] whereby States were invited to 'enhance understanding, coordination and cooperation with regard to climate change induced displacement, migration and planned relocation, where appropriate, at national, regional and international levels'; (ii) the Sendai Framework on Disaster Risk Reduction 2015–2030, which calls for the promotion of 'transboundary cooperation … to build resilience and reduce disaster risk, including … displacement risk';[178] and (iii) the ILC's Draft Articles on the Protection of Persons in the Event of Disasters which highlight the duty of affected States to seek assistance from the international community 'as appropriate',[179] refer to 'the fundamental value of solidarity in international relations and the importance of strengthening international cooperation in respect of all phases of a disaster',[180] and note that '[c]ooperation in the response to disasters includes humanitarian assistance,

---

174 On the activities of the fund, including for low-lying atoll States, see <http://www.greenclimate.fund> accessed 8 June 2018.

175 For a thorough analysis of the evolution of the principle of differential treatment in international environmental law between 1972 and 2012, see L. Rajamani, 'The Changing Fortunes of Differential Treatment in the Evolution of International Environmental Law' (2012) 88 *International Affairs* 605; D. Bodansky, 'The Paris Climate Change Agreement: A New Hope?' (2016) 110 *American Journal of International Law* 288.

176 See, e.g., UNFCCC, Kyoto Protocol to the United Nations Framework Convention on Climate Change (adopted 11 December 1997, entered into force 16 February 2005) 2303 UNTS 162 (Kyoto Protocol); Paris Agreement (adopted 12 December 2015, entered into force 4 November 2016) in Conference of the Parties, *Report of the Conference of the Parties on its twenty-first session, held in Paris from 30 November to 13 December 2015: Addendum: Part two: Action taken by the Conference of the Parties at its twenty-first session*, UN Doc. FCCC/CP/2015/10/Add.1 (29 January 2016) annex.

177 The Cancún Agreements: Outcome of the Work of the Ad Hoc Working Group on Long-term Cooperative Action under the Convention, in *Report of the Conference of the Parties on its sixteenth session, held in Cancun from 29 November to 10 December 2010, Addendum, Part Two: Action taken by the Conference of the Parties at its sixteenth session*, UN Doc. FCCC/CP/2010/7/Add.1 (15 March 2011) paras 11–35.

178 Sendai Framework (n. 143) para 28.

179 Draft Articles on the Protection of Persons in the Event of Disasters (n. 154), Article 11.

180 Ibid., Preamble.

coordination of international relief actions and communications, and making available relief personnel, equipment and goods, and scientific, medical and technical resources'.[181]

With respect to subparagraph (b) of Principle 4, paragraph 2, there are a number of national and regional examples of legislative and policy mechanisms addressing admission, stay (generally temporary), and/or status of those displaced in the context of disasters, generally based on humanitarian considerations.[182] They are largely *ad hoc*, uncoordinated, and unpredictable, and often based on discretionary considerations. The UNHCR's Guidelines on Temporary Protection and Stay Arrangements, published in February 2014, advocate for expanded and better coordinated temporary protection mechanisms,[183] with recommendations on admission, stay, and status for potential beneficiaries. At the regional level, examples such as the *Guide to Effective Practices for RCM Member Countries* create more harmonised responses for persons who are displaced by, or unable to return home on account of, the impacts of a disaster, recognising the mutual benefits that a

181 Ibid., Article 8. See also the Brazil Declaration, 'A Framework for Cooperation and Regional Solidarity to Strengthen the International Protection of Refugees, Displaced and Stateless Persons in Latin America and the Caribbean' (Brasilia, 3 December 2014) and UNGA, *One Humanity, Shared Responsibility: Report of the Secretary-General for the World Humanitarian Summit*, UN Doc. A/70/709 (2 February 2016) 55 which calls on States to: '[a]dopt an appropriate international framework, national legislation and regional cooperation frameworks by 2025 to ensure that countries in disaster-prone regions are prepared to receive and protect those displaced across borders without refugee status'.

182 See, e.g., D.J. Cantor, 'Law, Policy and Practice Concerning the Humanitarian Protection of Aliens on a Temporary Basis in the Context of Disasters: Background Paper: States of the Regional Conference on Migration and Others in the Americas, Regional Workshop on Temporary Protection Status and/or Humanitarian Visas in Situations of Disaster, San José', Costa Rica, 10–11 February 2015, 42–54 <http://disasterdisplacement.org/wp-content/uploads/2015/07/150715_FINAL_BACKGROUND_PAPER_LATIN_AMERICA_screen.pdf> accessed 8 June 2018; The Nansen Initiative (drafted for RCM Member Countries), *A Guide to Effective Practices for RCM Member Countries: Protection for persons moving across borders in the context of disasters* (Regional Conference for Migration 2016). In *AD (Tuvalu)* [2014] NZIPT 501370–371, protection was granted on humanitarian and discretionary grounds. Key factors influencing the decision included the fact that the appellant was the only sibling left in Tuvalu, he was the only son of the family, and there was a strong cultural need for him to be with his New Zealand-resident mother. While the effects of climate change and natural disasters were accepted to be a humanitarian circumstance within the meaning of the relevant statutory test, this was not the factor that determined the outcome.

183 UNHCR Division of International Protection, 'Guidelines on Temporary Protection or Stay Arrangements' (February 2014) <http://www.refworld.org/docid/52fba2404.html> accessed 8 June 2018.

more predictable response brings. Broadening access to temporary protection options – and creating more consistent and predictable responses in this regard – could help to address the protection needs of some persons displaced in the context of sea level rise.

However, temporary protection will not provide a solution in all cases. For example, where return is not possible, more durable solutions also need to be found. Existing national immigration laws and regulations related to employment, family, or education; other forms of privileged access to territory;[184] and regional free movement agreements, such as the Economic Union of the Organisation of Eastern Caribbean States, the Caribbean Single Market, and the Economic Community of West African States (ECOWAS), may present prospects for permanent migration, and/or might enable some forms of adaptive international migration, whether temporary or permanent.[185] For instance, new categories of visas could be created to enable persons to migrate with dignity before their homes become uninhabitable.

Principle 5 – Evacuation of Affected Persons

1. *States affected by sea level rise shall take all necessary measures to facilitate, without discrimination, the evacuation of persons facing a serious and imminent risk linked to the effects of sea level rise, and provide support to those unable to evacuate themselves.*
2. *Where evacuations are not voluntary, they shall only be undertaken if they are provided for by law and are necessary to protect the life and health of affected persons, and if less intrusive measures would be insufficient to avert the harmful consequences of the threat. Competent*

184 For example, in the aftermath of a series of earthquakes in Christchurch, New Zealand, the number of New Zealanders who left that area and moved to Australia was more than double the previous year (ca 3,600 versus ca 1,600). Their movement was facilitated by the Trans-Tasman Travel Arrangement, which enables Australian and New Zealand citizens (without health or character concerns) to visit, live and work in either country indefinitely and without restrictions. This provided a ready 'self-help' mechanism that enabled persons to plan for their future, rather than leaving them without a solution or reliant on a hastily conceived *ad hoc* response. See, e.g., P. Lafferty, 'International Migration to/from Christchurch after the Earthquakes' (PowerPoint Presentation, PANZ Conference, 29 November 2011), at <http://www.population.org.nz/wp-content/uploads/2012/02/3b3_peter-lafferty.pdf> last accessed 8 June 2018.

185 Family reunification may provide greater scope for permanent international migration through sponsorship and other mechanisms. See generally The Nansen Initiative (n. 151) paras 46–63, 87–93, 119–20.

authorities should ensure that evacuation orders are enforced only for as long as strictly necessary to fulfil such purpose.

3. *Evacuations, whether voluntary or forced, shall be carried out with full respect for the life, dignity, liberty, and security of evacuees.*

Commentary

The duty to protect the right to life may oblige States to evacuate persons at imminent risk of harm from storm surges, flooding, and other life-threatening hazards associated with sea level rise.[186] This entails the duty to facilitate voluntary evacuations, as well as to order forced evacuations where this is the only way to save lives.

Where evacuations are not voluntary, a tension arises between the State's duty to protect life, on the one hand, and the individual's right to liberty of movement and freedom to choose one's residence[187] – which also encompasses the right to stay[188] – on the other. Paragraph 2 of Principle 5 lists the permissible limitations on the right to stay.[189] Paragraph 3 of Principle 5 is based on the UN Guiding Principles on Internal Displacement.[190]

Principle 6 – Planned Relocations of Affected Persons

1. *States affected by sea level rise shall only undertake planned relocations (whether within their territories or across international borders) when*

186 See in particular *Budayeva* (n. 166) paras 148ff.

187 ICCPR, Article 12; Protocol No. 4 to the Convention for the Protection of Human Rights and Fundamental Freedoms, Securing Certain Rights and Freedoms Other Than Those Already Included in the Convention and in the First Protocol Thereto, Strasbourg, 16.IX.1963, ETS No. 46 (entered into force 2 May 1968), as amended by Protocol No. 11, ETS No 155 (Protocol 4 to ECHR), Article 2; Universal Declaration of Human Rights (adopted 10 December 1948) UNGA res 217 A(III) (UDHR) Article 13.

188 HRC General Comment No. 27 'Freedom of movement (article 12)', UN Doc. CCPR/C/21/Rev.1/Add.9 (1 November 1999) para 7: 'Subject to the provisions of article 12, paragraph 3, the right to reside in a place of one's choice within the territory includes protection against all forms of forced internal displacement'.

189 See ICCPR, Article 12(3). See also Guiding Principles on Internal Displacement (n. 148) principle 6(2)(d).

190 Guiding Principles on Internal Displacement (n. 148) principle 8. See also principle 7(2), providing that authorities undertaking displacement, including through evacuation, 'shall ensure, to the greatest practicable extent, that proper accommodation is provided to displaced persons, that such displacements are effected in satisfactory conditions of safety, nutrition, health and hygiene, and that members of the same family are not separated'.

so requested by affected persons and communities, or when conducted with their full, free, and informed consent.

2. *Where, despite the provision of adequate information and consultation, such consent cannot be obtained, planned relocations must only be undertaken as a measure of last resort to safeguard the lives and safety of those affected. They must be based on national law and implemented in accordance with relevant international legal standards.*
3. *Planned relocations shall be implemented in ways that safeguard the human rights and dignity of those who move, including the principle of family unity, as well as the human rights and dignity of those who receive relocated persons.*
4. *Given their significance for indigenous peoples, States undertaking planned relocation shall respect and protect their rights to self-determination, culture, identity, land, and resources.*
5. *Persons affected by a planned relocation, including those who receive relocated persons, must be informed, consulted, allowed, and enabled to participate in all relevant decision-making processes.*
6. *At a minimum, persons' pre-relocation living standards must be restored post-relocation.*

Commentary

As a preventive measure, planned relocations can help persons move away from dangerous areas in advance of anticipated disasters or longer-term environmental degradation. They may provide a durable solution for persons who were displaced or evacuated in the context of a sudden-onset event by resettling them in safer areas if return home is not possible.[191] However, planned relocations are not a panacea and must be approached with considerable care and caution. Relocation is a complex and fraught process, requiring in-depth consultation and planning to avoid greater vulnerability, impoverishment, and social fragmentation.[192] This is borne out in numerous internal relocations that have occurred (primarily in the context of development projects),[193] as

191 The Nansen Initiative (n. 151) paras 94–98, 121–22.

192 See, e.g., E. Ferris, 'Protection and Planned Relocations in the Context of Climate Change' (August 2012), *UNHCR Legal and Protection Policy Research Series*, PPLA/2012/04; A.R. Thomas, 'Post-disaster resettlement in the Philippines: A risky strategy' (2015) 49 *Forced Migration Review* 52; J. McAdam and E. Ferris, 'Planned Relocations in the Context of Climate Change: Unpacking the Legal and Conceptual Issues' (2015) 4 *Cambridge Journal of International and Comparative Law* 137.

193 See, e.g., Ferris (n. 192).

well as in the handful of cross-border relocations (which have taken place in the Pacific).[194]

If planned relocation becomes a necessary and viable option, policymakers will need to pay acute attention to planning, embrace lessons learned from past experiences, prioritise a human rights-centred approach throughout the process, and ensure that relocations occur with the free and informed consent of the communities concerned (unless they are the only means to save lives). There are also questions about how to balance the human rights of relocated groups with those of the communities into which they move. The Sendai Framework, for example, encourages 'the adoption of policies and programmes addressing disaster-induced human mobility to strengthen the resilience of affected people and that of host communities'.[195]

While international case law on planned relocation is scarce,[196] relevant expert guidance is available.[197]

Principle 7 – Migration of Affected Persons

1. *States should recognise that temporary, circular, or permanent migration across borders can be an important means for persons to adapt to climate change and cope with the adverse effects of sea level rise.*
2. *Both States of origin and destination should review existing domestic laws, as well as bilateral and regional migration arrangements, and consider new laws and agreements, to facilitate migration as an adaptation measure, in accordance with applicable international human rights law as well as international labour law.*

194 See J. McAdam, 'Historical Cross-Border Relocation in the Pacific: Lessons for Planned Relocations in the Context of Climate Change' (2014) 49 *The Journal of Pacific History* 301.

195 Sendai Framework (n. 143) para 30.

196 See, however, on relocation as a consequence of development projects, *Centre for Minority Rights Development (Kenya) and Minority Rights Group International on behalf of Endorois Welfare Council v Kenya*, App No. 276/2003, African Commission on Human and Peoples' Rights.

197 Guidance on Planned Relocation (n. 152) principles 5–8; UNHCR/Georgetown University/IOM, 'A Toolbox: Planning Relocations to Protect People from Disasters and Environmental Change' (2017) <http://www.unhcr.org/596f1bb47.pdf> accessed 8 June 2018; 'The Peninsula Principles on Climate Displacement within States' (2013) <http://displacement-solutions.org/wp-content/uploads/2014/12/Peninsula-Principles.pdf> accessed 8 June 2018. See also UN General Assembly, *Protection of and Assistance to Internally Displaced Persons: Note by Secretary-General* (transmitting the Report of the Special Rapporteur on the Human Rights of Internally Displaced Persons, Chaloka Beyani, in accordance with General Assembly Resolution 64/142 and Human Rights Council Resolution 14/6, UN Doc. A/66/285) (9 August 2011) paras 61ff.

3. *Both States of origin and destination should cooperate to ensure that the full range of rights and protections afforded to migrants by international law is respected, including the right to liberty of movement and the freedom to choose one's place of residence.*

Commentary

Migration can be an effective way to build the long-term resilience of persons and communities, allowing them to cope with the adverse impacts of sea level rise and potentially reduce or avoid displacement at a later stage. Temporary or circular[198] migration can be a beneficial channel for livelihood diversification when living conditions in low-lying coastal areas become difficult. Remittances, as well as knowledge acquired abroad, have the potential to increase significantly the resilience of communities living in such areas. Temporary or permanent migration often occurs in the aftermath of a disaster when internally displaced persons or those otherwise affected conclude that protection, assistance, and recovery measures are insufficient in their area or State of origin. Permanent migration may be the only option for those who anticipate that, in the long-term, their homes will become uninhabitable or lost as a consequence of sea level rise. It may allow them to maintain some degree of agency over when and where to go, before displacement becomes inevitable.

Whether anticipatory or reactive, migration as a coping or adaptation strategy may be highly beneficial in the context of sea level rise, provided that persons can migrate with dignity and that their human rights are respected by all States involved in the migration process. Therefore, proactively anticipating and planning for migration is an important policy measure. Migration can enable persons to move away from the impacts of sea level rise voluntarily, on their own terms, and relatively safely, and can play an important role in risk management strategies. Increased migration may also help to relieve population and resource pressures in areas of origin, particularly in some low-lying island States where these are of pressing concern.[199]

The option of migration as a form of adaptation has been recognised by States parties to the UNFCCC.[200] However, international law does not explicitly address the right of admission and stay of persons who migrate in anticipation of, or in response to, disasters. Thus, the extent to which persons can migrate

198 While there is no one settled definition, circular migration is typically understood as referring to recurrent temporary migration between two or more countries, often for work or study purposes.

199 McAdam, *Climate Change, Forced Migration, and International Law* (n. 146) 204.

200 Cancún Adaptation Framework (n. 143) para 14(f).

voluntarily depends upon the legal and policy frameworks in place, and the resources available to them. In particular, the creation of domestic legal frameworks will play a significant role in determining the extent to which persons affected by adverse effects of sea level rise may move abroad and remain there.

In order to make migration a realistic and manageable option, States of destination should review or amend their domestic laws to facilitate such migration, building on existing good practices[201] in the spirit of the principle of common but differentiated responsibilities. Bilateral or regional migration arrangements on the free movement of persons are another effective tool to ensure that movement is safe, orderly, and regular.[202]

While migration as an adaptation and coping strategy can be beneficial, it also carries the risk of exploitation, trafficking, or discrimination, amongst other things. For this reason, it is essential to ensure full respect for the rights of migrants as enshrined in applicable international human rights[203] and international labour law.

Principle 8 – Internal Displacement of Affected Persons

States shall protect and assist persons displaced within their territory in the context of sea level rise and associated hazards and establish conditions for, as well as provide the means which allow internally displaced persons to find, durable solutions, in accordance with the UN Guiding Principles on Internal Displacement.

201 See The Nansen Initiative (vol I) (n. 151) para 88 and The Nansen Initiative, *Agenda for the Protection of Cross-Border Displaced Persons in the Context of Disasters and Climate Change* (vol II, December 2015) <http://disasterdisplacement.org/wp-content/uploads/2015/02/PROTECTION-AGENDA-VOLUME-2.pdf> accessed 8 June 2018, 42–48.

202 To ensure safe, orderly and regular migration is the goal of the Global Compact for Migration to be adopted in December 2018. To what extent the Compact will address migration in the context of sea level rise remains to be seen.

203 Besides the International Convention on the Protection of the Rights of All Migrant Workers and Members of Their Families (adopted 18 December 1990, entered into force 1 July 2003) 2220 UNTS 3, the ICESCR, ICCPR, International Convention on the Elimination of all Forms of Racial Discrimination (adopted 7 March 1966, entered into force 4 January 1969) 660 UNTS 195, and the Convention on the Elimination of All Forms of Discrimination against Women (adopted 18 December 1979, entered into force 3 September 1981) 1249 UNTS 13 (CEDAW) are particularly relevant.

Commentary

The Guiding Principles are recognised as 'an important international framework for the protection of internally displaced persons'[204] and encompass persons 'who have been forced or obliged to flee or to leave their homes or places of habitual residence, in particular as a result of or in order to avoid the effects of ... natural or human-made disasters, and who have not crossed an internationally recognized State border'.[205] Despite being non-binding, they are based upon and reflect binding international law and thus provide detailed guidance for the protection and assistance of persons displaced within their own countries in the context of sea level rise.[206]

In order to make the Guiding Principles effective, they need to be integrated into domestic laws and policies. Authorities also need to have sufficient capacity and resources to make them operational (see Principle 3, paragraph 2 above).

Principle 9 – Cross-Border Displacement of Affected Persons

1. *States should admit persons displaced across borders in the context of disasters linked to sea level rise if they are personally and seriously at risk of, or already affected by, a disaster, or if their State of origin is unable to protect and assist them due to the disaster (even if temporarily). States should ensure that they have adequate laws and policies in place to facilitate this protection.*
2. *States of refuge should not return persons to territories where they face a serious risk to their life or safety or serious hardship, in particular due to the fact that they cannot access necessary humanitarian assistance or protection. In all cases, States must observe the prohibition on forcible return to situations of persecution or other forms of serious harm, as provided for by applicable international law.*

---

204 See '2005 World Summit Outcome', UNGA res 60/1 (24 October 2005) para 132 and subsequent resolutions by the General Assembly (including UNGA res 70/165 (22 February 2016) para 7 and UNGA res 68/180 (30 January 2014) para 16) and the Human Rights Council (including 'Mandate of the Special Rapporteur on the human rights of internally displaced persons', HRC res 23/8 (20 June 2013) para 12).

205 Guiding Principles on Internal Displacement (n. 148). Similarly, see the African Union Convention for the Protection and Assistance of Internally Displaced Persons in Africa (Kampala Convention) (adopted 23 October 2009, entered into force 6 December 2012) I-52375, Article 1.

206 See *Protection of and Assistance to Internally Displaced Persons* (n. 197) paras 18–86.

3. *States that have admitted cross-border disaster-displaced persons should cooperate with States of origin to find durable solutions for such persons. This may include return where possible, or permanent admission and stay in the host State.*
4. *States ready to admit cross-border disaster-displaced persons should strive to harmonise their practices regarding the admission and protection of cross-border disaster-displaced persons at the regional and/or sub-regional levels.*

Commentary

Persons displaced across borders in the context of disasters linked to sea level rise do not qualify as refugees *per se*. However, many States have used their discretion in migration matters to admit cross-border disaster displaced persons at least on a temporary basis, and to refrain from removing foreigners who were present on their territory at the time of the disaster, even if their visas have expired. Such admission has been based on: (i) regional or bilateral agreements on free movement of persons; (ii) regular national migration laws; (iii) exceptional migration categories, such as humanitarian visas or temporary protection status; and (iv) *ad hoc* decisions.

An analysis of such practices[207] indicates that States are willing to admit or refrain from returning persons who are seriously and personally affected by the disaster, particularly because: (i) an on-going or, in rare cases, an imminent and foreseeable disaster in the country of origin poses a real risk to their life or safety; (ii) as a direct result of the disaster, they have been wounded, lost family members, and/or lost their livelihoods; and/or (iii) they would face a real risk to their life or safety or would otherwise face very serious hardship in their country of origin, in particular due to the fact that they cannot access necessary humanitarian protection and assistance there. States may also grant admission to, or refrain from returning persons who originate from States whose government capacity to respond is temporarily overwhelmed due to the disaster.[208]

As reflected in paragraph 2 of Principle 9, international and regional refugee and human rights law prohibits the removal of persons to a real risk of persecution or other serious harm, such as inhuman or degrading treatment. In refugee law, while the underlying disaster or climate change process will not constitute 'persecution' *per se*, it may provide a context in which forms

207 The Nansen Initiative (vol II) (n. 201) 40–41; Cantor (n. 182).

208 The Nansen Initiative (vol I) (n. 151) para 33; *A Guide to Effective Practices for RCM Member Countries* (n. 182) 16.

of harm that do engage existing international protection regimes may arise – for instance, where the disaster causes a breakdown of law and order[209] or is used by a government as pretext for persecutory acts against certain parts of the population.[210] Regional human rights law has acknowledged that return to situations of very serious destitution or dire humanitarian conditions may amount to cruel, inhuman, or degrading treatment.[211]

While in practice, admission or non-return in the aftermath of a disaster is usually temporary in nature, it is important to find durable solutions that bring displacement to an end, either through return and reintegration in the State of origin or via permanent admission to the host State. The latter might become particularly relevant in the future if large parts of low-lying atoll States become permanently uninhabitable or inundated. In this context, international cooperation (see Principle 4) will be particularly relevant (see Principle 9, paragraph 3).

---

209 Because of their reference to 'serious disruption of public order' as a reason for granting refugee status, the African Refugee Convention and the Cartagena Declaration have the potential to cover situations of climate change-related cross-border displacement as well. See Organization of African Unity Convention Governing the Specific Aspects of Refugee Problems in Africa of 10 September 1969 (adopted 10 September 1969, entered into force 20 June 1974) 1001 UNTS 45, para 1(2) and Cartagena Declaration on Refugees (adopted by the Colloquium on the International Protection of Refugees in Central America, Mexico, and Panama, 22 November 1984) in Annual Report of the Inter-American Commission on Human Rights (1984–85), OAS Doc. OEA/Ser.L/V/II.66/doc.10, rev 1, 190–93.

210 Judicial bodies, particularly in New Zealand, have begun to map the contours of applicability of international refugee and human rights law to disaster situations in a series of cases. See *AF (Kiribati)* [2013] NZIPT 800413 (25 June 2013). Upheld on appeal in *Teitiota v The Chief Executive of the Ministry of Business, Innovation and Employment* [2013] NZHC 3125 (26 November 2013), *Teitiota v The Chief Executive of Ministry of Business, Innovation and Employment* [2014] NZCA 173 (8 May 2014), *Teitiota v The Chief Executive of the Ministry of Business, Innovation and Employment* [2015] NZSC 107 (20 July 2015), and *AC (Tuvalu)* (n. 169).

211 See e.g. *MSS v Belgium and Greece*, App No. 30696/09 (Grand Chamber, 21 January 2011) para 249; *Sufi and Elmi v United Kingdom*, App Nos 8319/07 and 11449/07 (28 June 2011). The Inter-American Court of Human Rights has held that the right to life enshrines a duty 'of generating minimum living conditions that are compatible with the dignity of the human person and of not creating conditions that hinder or impede it,' but it has not yet had an opportunity to examine whether this would entail a prohibition of return to situations of humanitarian emergencies where adequate humanitarian protection and assistance is not available or accessible. See Judgment, *Yakye Axa Indigenous Community v Paraguay* (17 June 2005), Series C No. 125, para 162, referring to Judgment, *Case of the 'Juvenile Reeducation Institute'* (2 September 2004), Series C No. 112, para 159.

A particular problem with current State practice is its uneven application and lack of predictability. In the absence of binding international law, the harmonisation of effective practices on admission and protection is of paramount importance and is best done at the regional and sub-regional levels, for instance within the framework of regional conferences or dialogues on migration (see Principle 9, paragraph 4).[212]

Annexes

Resolution 5/2018: Committee on International Law and Sea Level Rise

The 78th Conference of the International Law Association, held in Sydney, Australia, 19–24 August 2018:

HAVING CONSIDERED the Report of the Committee on International Law and Sea Level Rise submitted to the 78th Conference, as well as taking note of the Interim Report of the Committee submitted to the 77th Conference held in Johannesburg, South Africa, in 2016;

APPRECIATING that sea level rise is likely to have a major impact on the coastal features from which maritime zones are measured, causing uncertainties as to the determination of the breadth and extent of maritime zones in accordance with the law of the sea, as well as possible uncertainties regarding agreed or adjudicated maritime boundaries;

ENDORSES the views of the Committee that:
- any proposals in this area should aim to facilitate orderly relations between States and, ultimately, the avoidance of conflicts, bearing in mind that one of the principal motivations of the United Nations Convention on the Law of the Sea is to contribute to the maintenance of international peace and security; and
- in the formulation of proposals for the progressive development of international law, the dominant considerations should be the need to avoid uncertainty about the extent and limits of maritime zones and location of boundaries and to avoid

212 See *A Guide to Effective Practices* (n. 182) as an example of harmonisation work undertaken in the Central/North American region. A similar exercise was started in 2017 in South America. Regional Conferences on Migration also exist in other regions affected by sea level rise.

incentives artificially to preserve baselines physically in order to keep the outer limits of maritime zones;

NOTES that the Committee has presented evidence of the emergence of State practice, particularly in the South Pacific region, indicating that small island States intend to maintain the baselines and limits of their current maritime zones established in accordance with the 1982 Law of the Sea Convention for the future, notwithstanding physical coastline changes brought about by sea level rise;

ENDORSES the proposal of the Committee that, on the grounds of legal certainty and stability, provided that the baselines and the outer limits of maritime zones of a coastal or an archipelagic State have been properly determined in accordance with the 1982 Law of the Sea Convention, these baselines and limits should not be required to be recalculated should sea level change affect the geographical reality of the coastline;

ENDORSES ALSO the Committee's proposal that the interpretation of the 1982 Law of the Sea Convention in relation to the ability of coastal and archipelagic States to maintain their existing lawful maritime entitlements should apply equally to maritime boundaries delimited by international agreement or by decisions of international courts or arbitral tribunals;

CONFIRMS that the Committee's recommendations regarding the maintenance of existing maritime entitlements are conditional upon the coastal State's existing maritime claims having been made in compliance with the requirements of the 1982 Law of the Sea Convention and duly published or notified to the Secretary-General of the United Nations as required by the relevant provisions of the Convention, prior to physical coastline changes brought about by sea level rise;

REQUESTS the Secretary-General of the International Law Association to forward this Resolution to the Secretary-General of the United Nations with the request that it be brought to the attention of States Parties to the United Nations Convention on the Law of the Sea, other interested States, and the International Law Commission;

ALSO REQUESTS the Secretary-General of the International Law Association to forward this Resolution to the Registrar of the International Court of Justice, the Registrar of the International Tribunal for the Law of the Sea, and the Secretary-General of the Permanent Court of Arbitration.

Resolution 6/2018: Committee on International Law and Sea Level Rise

The 78th Conference of the International Law Association, held in Sydney, Australia, 19–24 August 2018:

HAVING CONSIDERED the two reports of the Committee on International Law and Sea Level Rise (2016 and 2018) covering, inter alia, the issue of displacement of persons in the context of sea level rise and the identification of emerging principles of international law relating to the protection of persons displaced in the context of sea level rise;

TAKING NOTE of the findings documented in the Fifth Assessment Report of the Intergovernmental Panel on Climate Change in 2014, predicting an increase of sea levels ranging between 26 cm and 98 cm above 1990 levels by 2100;

RECOGNISING the need for an effective response to the urgent threats posed by sea level rise;

CONCERNED by the impacts that sea level rise already has on low-lying islands and coastal areas, which are often densely populated;

RECOGNISING that sea level rise will jeopardise further the habitability of such areas in the decades to come, creating a potentially large number of persons displaced from areas affected by sea level rise;

RECOGNISING ALSO that some of the affected populations may be forced to leave their homes to find assistance and protection abroad;

RECALLING the Malé Declaration on Global Warming and Sea Level Rise adopted by the Small States Conference on Sea Level Rise, held at Malé, Maldives, from 14 to 18 November 1989, in which the participants declared their intent to work, collaborate and seek international cooperation to protect the low-lying small coastal and island States from the dangers posed by climate change, global warming and sea level rise;

RECALLING ALSO General Assembly Resolution 44/206 of 22 December 1989 on the possible adverse effects of sea level rise on islands and coastal areas, in which UN Member States urged the international community to provide effective and timely support to States affected by sea level rise, particularly developing States, in their efforts to develop and implement strategies to protect themselves and their vulnerable natural marine ecosystems from the particular threats of sea level rise caused by climate change;

RECALLING ALSO General Assembly Resolution 70/1 of 25 September 2015 on the 2030 Agenda for Sustainable Development highlighting that increases in global temperature, sea level rise, ocean acidification and other climate change impacts are seriously affecting coastal areas and low-lying coastal States, including many least developed States and small island developing States;

CONVINCED that the treatment of persons displaced in the context of sea level rise should be based on and guided by international legal principles;

MINDFUL of the fact that such principles can be derived from a multitude of existing legal provisions and frameworks;

RECOGNISING the recent efforts of the international community to develop further a comprehensive legal and policy framework for the protection of people displaced in the face of climate change, including through the adoption of the Agenda for the Protection of Cross-Border Displaced Persons in the Context of Disasters and Climate Change (Protection Agenda), endorsed by 109 governmental delegations during a global intergovernmental consultation on 12–13 October 2015 in Geneva, and the Global Compact for Migration to be adopted in December 2018;

ADOPTS the Sydney Declaration of Principles on the Protection of Persons Displaced in the Context of Sea Level Rise annexed to this Resolution;

REQUESTS the Secretary-General of the International Law Association to forward this Resolution, along with the Declaration of Principles annexed to it, to the UN Secretary-General, the UNFCCC Secretariat, the Chair of the Executive Committee of the Warsaw International Mechanism for Loss and Damage associated with Climate Change Impacts and its Task Force on Displacement, the Special Representative of the UN Secretary-General for International Migration, the Co-Facilitators to lead the intergovernmental consultations and negotiations on issues related to the Global Compact for Safe, Orderly and Regular Migration, the Director of the International Organization for Migration, the UN High Commissioner for Refugees, and the Platform on Disaster Displacement for their consideration;

RECOMMENDS to the Executive Council to extend the mandate of the Committee on International Law and Sea Level Rise in order for the Committee to continue its work on the remaining aspects of its mandate.

Sydney Declaration of Principles on the Protection of Persons Displaced in the Context of Sea Level Rise

Purpose

The purpose of the present Declaration of Principles is to provide guidance to States in averting, mitigating, and addressing displacement of persons occurring in the context of sea level rise, based on and derived from relevant international legal provisions, principles, and frameworks.

Scope

The present Declaration of Principles applies to all forms of human mobility arising in the context of sea level rise.

Definitions

For the purposes of the present Declaration of Principles, the following definitions shall apply:

(a) 'disaster' means a serious disruption of the functioning of a community or a society at any scale, due to climatic events interacting with conditions of exposure, vulnerability, and capacity, leading to human, material, economic, and/or environmental losses and impacts;

(b) 'displacement' means the movement within a State and/or across international borders of persons who are forced or obliged to leave their homes or places of habitual residence due to sudden-onset natural hazards and/or slower, cumulative pressures occurring in the context of sea level rise;

(c) 'evacuation' means the rapid movement of persons away from the immediate threat or impact of a disaster to a place of shelter, in order to ensure their security, safety, and well-being;

(d) 'human mobility' means all relevant forms of the movement of persons in the context of sea level rise, including displacement, evacuation, migration, and planned relocation;

(e) 'migration' means predominantly voluntary cross-border movement, which, in the context of disaster- and climate change-related impacts, is more likely to occur in anticipation of future harm;

(f) 'planned relocation' means a planned process in which persons voluntarily move or are forced to move away from their homes or places of temporary residence, are settled in a new location within their own or another State, and are provided with the conditions for rebuilding their lives. Planned relocation is carried out under the authority of the State, and is undertaken to protect persons from risks and impacts related to disasters and environmental change in the context of sea level rise;

(g) 'sea level rise' means the sole or combined and cumulative impacts of the effects of climate change and subsidence or land uplift on the change of the sea level in a given location.

Principle 1 – The Primary Duty and Responsibility of States to Protect and Assist Affected Persons

States have the primary duty and responsibility to provide protection and assistance to persons with habitual residence in territories under their jurisdiction who are affected by sea level rise.

Principle 2 – The Duty to Respect the Human Rights of Affected Persons

States of origin, transit, and destination have a duty to respect, on a non-discriminatory basis, the human rights of persons under their jurisdiction who move in the context of sea level rise, including:

(a) their right to liberty of movement and freedom to choose their residence;
(b) the freedom to leave and return to their own country;
(c) their right to be protected against *refoulement*;
(d) their right to be informed and consulted, and to participate in decisions affecting them;
(e) the cultural and land rights of indigenous peoples and local communities.

Principle 3 – The Duty to Take Positive Action

1. States have a duty to use the best practicable means at their disposal, in accordance with their respective capabilities and resources and their international human rights obligations, as well as other relevant international standards and frameworks, to take appropriate and effective measures, including those referred to in Principles 5–9, to:
   (a) reduce disaster risks and adapt to the adverse effects of climate change in order to protect the lives and ensure the safety of persons with habitual residence on low-lying areas at risk of sea level rise under their jurisdiction;
   (b) prevent displacement of such persons; and
   (c) protect and assist them in the event of displacement.
2. In order to avert, mitigate, and address displacement in the context of sea level rise, and to protect and assist persons displaced in this context, States should, in particular:

(a) adopt adequate normative frameworks and operational measures to implement them;
(b) assign powers and responsibilities to competent authorities and institutions or, where they do not exist, create such authorities and institutions endowed with appropriate powers and responsibilities; and
(c) provide adequate resources to such authorities and institutions.

Principle 4 – The Duty to Cooperate

1. States shall enhance international cooperation among themselves and with relevant international organisations and agencies to assist States affected by sea level rise to prevent, avoid, and respond to disaster- and climate change-related risks, including the risk of displacement. Affected States should call on the international community when they require assistance.
2. Cooperation in this context may include:
   (a) efforts at bilateral, regional and/or sub-regional levels to strengthen and coordinate measures to:
      i. reduce disaster risk, enhance adaptation to climate change, and build resilience of affected communities living in low-lying areas at risk of sea level rise;
      ii. assist, in accordance with elementary humanitarian considerations, in the evacuation of persons where necessary to save lives, including across borders;
      iii. facilitate cross-border migration in anticipation of, or in reaction to, irreversible environmental degradation or sudden-onset disasters linked to sea level rise;
      iv. enhance the humanitarian response in situations of internal displacement; and
      v. support recovery, including durable solutions, for internally displaced persons;
   (b) efforts to ensure that persons moving across borders are admitted and received with respect for their safety, dignity, and human rights, including the creation or harmonisation of more predictable domestic or regional legal frameworks, and that durable solutions to displacement are found; and
   (c) technical and financial support by the international community and donor States and their multilateral and bilateral financing mechanisms to support affected States and regions.

Principle 5 – Evacuation of Affected Persons

1. States affected by sea level rise shall take all necessary measures to facilitate, without discrimination, the evacuation of persons facing a serious and imminent risk linked to the effects of sea level rise, and provide support to those unable to evacuate themselves.
2. Where evacuations are not voluntary, they shall only be undertaken if they are provided for by law and are necessary to protect the life and health of affected persons, and if less intrusive measures would be insufficient to avert the harmful consequences of the threat. Competent authorities should ensure that evacuation orders are enforced only for as long as strictly necessary to fulfil such purpose.
3. Evacuations, whether voluntary or forced, shall be carried out with full respect for the life, dignity, liberty, and security of evacuees.

Principle 6 – Planned Relocations of Affected Persons

1. States affected by sea level rise shall only undertake planned relocations (whether within their territories or across international borders) when so requested by affected persons and communities, or when conducted with their full, free, and informed consent.
2. Where, despite the provision of adequate information and consultation, such consent cannot be obtained, planned relocations must only be undertaken as a measure of last resort to safeguard the lives and safety of those affected. They must be based on national law and implemented in accordance with relevant international legal standards.
3. Planned relocations shall be implemented in ways that safeguard the human rights and dignity of those who move, including the principle of family unity, as well as the human rights and dignity of those who receive relocated persons.
4. Given their significance for indigenous peoples, States undertaking planned relocation shall respect and protect their rights to self-determination, culture, identity, land, and resources.
5. Persons affected by a planned relocation, including those who receive relocated persons, must be informed, consulted, allowed, and enabled to participate in all relevant decision-making processes.
6. At a minimum, persons' pre-relocation living standards must be restored post-relocation.

Principle 7 – Migration of Affected Persons

1. States should recognise that temporary, circular, or permanent migration across borders can be an important means for persons to adapt to climate change and cope with the adverse effects of sea level rise.

2. Both States of origin and destination should review existing domestic laws, as well as bilateral and regional migration arrangements, and consider new laws and agreements, to facilitate migration as an adaptation measure, in accordance with applicable international human rights law as well as international labour law.
3. Both States of origin and destination should cooperate to ensure that the full range of rights and protections afforded to migrants by international law is respected, including the right to liberty of movement and the freedom to choose one's place of residence.

Principle 8 – Internal Displacement of Affected Persons

States shall protect and assist persons displaced within their territory in the context of sea level rise and associated hazards and establish conditions for, as well as provide the means which allow internally displaced persons to find, durable solutions, in accordance with the UN Guiding Principles on Internal Displacement.

Principle 9 – Cross-Border Displacement of Affected Persons

1. States should admit persons displaced across borders in the context of disasters linked to sea level rise if they are personally and seriously at risk of, or already affected by, a disaster, or if their State of origin is unable to protect and assist them due to the disaster (even if temporarily). States should ensure that they have adequate laws and policies in place to facilitate this protection.
2. States of refuge should not return persons to territories where they face a serious risk to their life or safety or serious hardship, in particular due to the fact that they cannot access necessary humanitarian assistance or protection. In all cases, States must observe the prohibition on forcible return to situations of persecution or other forms of serious harm, as provided for by applicable international law.
3. States that have admitted cross-border disaster-displaced persons should cooperate with States of origin to find durable solutions for such persons. This may include return where possible, or permanent admission and stay in the host State.
4. States ready to admit cross-border disaster-displaced persons should strive to harmonise their practices regarding the admission and protection of cross-border disaster-displaced persons at the regional and/or sub-regional levels.

References

Adger, W.N., et al., 'Human Security', in: *Climate Change 2014: Impacts, Adaptation, and Vulnerability, Part A: Global and Sectoral Aspects. Contribution of Working Group II to the Fifth Assessment Report of the Intergovernmental Panel on Climate Change* (Cambridge University Press, 2014), 775–791.

Arnadottir, S., 'Termination of Maritime Boundaries Due to a Fundamental Change of Circumstances' (2016) 32 *Utrecht Journal of International and European Law* 94–111.

Bird, E., and J. Prescott, 'Rising Global Sea Levels and National Maritime Claims', (1989) 1 *Marine Policy Reports* 177–196.

Bodansky, D., 'The Paris Climate Change Agreement: A New Hope?' (2016) 110 *American Journal of International Law* 288–319.

Brookings/Georgetown University/UNHCR, 'Guidance on Protecting People from Disasters and Environmental Change through Planned Relocation' (7 October 2015), available at: <https://www.brookings.edu/wp-content/uploads/2016/06/GUIDANCE_PLANNED-RELOCATION_14-OCT-2015.pdf> (last accessed 8 June 2018).

Camp Coordination and Camp Management Cluster, 'The MEND Guide: Comprehensive Guide for Planning Mass Evacuations in Natural Disasters: Pilot Document', 16–17, available at: <http://www.globalcccmcluster.org/tools-and-guidance/publications/mend-guide> (last accessed 8 June 2018).

Cantor, D.J., 'Law, Policy and Practice Concerning the Humanitarian Protection of Aliens on a Temporary Basis in the Context of Disasters. Background Paper: States of the Regional Conference on Migration and Others in the Americas, Regional Workshop on Temporary Protection Status and/or Humanitarian Visas in Situations of Disaster, San José', Costa Rica, 10–11 February 2015, 42–54; available at <http://disasterdisplacement.org/wp-content/uploads/2015/07/150715_FINAL_BACKGROUND_PAPER_LATIN_AMERICA_screen.pdf> (last accessed 8 June 2018).

Caron, D.D., 'When Law Makes Climate Change Worse: Rethinking the Law of Baselines in Light of Rising Sea Level' (1990) 17 *Ecology Law Quarterly* 621–653.

Caron, D.D., 'Climate Change, Sea Level Rise and the Coming Uncertainty in Oceanic Boundaries: A Proposal to Avoid Conflict', in: S-Y. Hong and J.M. Van Dyke (eds), *Maritime Boundary Disputes, Settlement Processes, and the Law of the Sea* (Leiden/Boston: Martinus Nijhoff, 2009), 1–17.

Charney, J.I., and L.M. Alexander (eds), *International Maritime Boundaries*, Vol. I (Dordrecht/Boston/London: Martinus Nijhoff, 1993).

Church, J.A., et al., 'Sea Level Change', in: *Climate Change 2013: The Physical Science Basis. Contribution of Working Group I to the Fifth Assessment Report of the Intergovernmental Panel on Climate Change* (Cambridge University Press, 2013), 1137–1216.

Committee on Economic, Social and Cultural Rights, CESCR General Comment No. 2 (1990) 'International technical assistance measures (Article 22 of the Covenant)', in Committee on Economic, Social and Cultural Rights, *Report on the Fourth Session (15 January–2 February 1990)*, Economic and Social Council Official Records, 1990, Supp No. 3 (E/1990/23) annex III.

Committee on Economic, Social and Cultural Rights, CESCR General Comment No. 3 (1990) 'The nature of States parties obligations (Art. 2, para 1 of the Covenant)', in Committee on Economic, Social and Cultural Rights, *Report on the Fifth Session (26 November–14 December 1990)*, Economic and Social Council Official Records, 1991, Supp No 3 (E/1991/23) annex III.

Committee on Economic, Social and Cultural Rights, CESCR General Comment No. 14 (2000) 'The right to the highest attainable standard of health (Article 12 of the International Covenant on Economic, Social and Cultural Rights)', UN Doc. E/C.12/2000/4 (11 August 2000).

Committee on Economic, Social and Cultural Rights, CESCR 'General Comment 12: The Right to Adequate Food (Art. 11)', UN Doc. E/C.12/1999/5 (12 May 1999) para 13; CESCR General Comment No 15 (2002) 'The right to water (arts 11 and 12 of the International Covenant on Economic, Social and Cultural Rights)', UN Doc. E/C.12/2002/11 (20 January 2003).

Crutzen, P., and E. Stoermer, 'The Anthropocene' (2000) 41 *Global Change Newsletter* 17–18.

Crutzen, P., 'Geology of Mankind' (2002) 415 *Nature* 23.

DeConto, R.M., and D. Pollard, 'Contribution of Antarctica to past and future sea-level rise' (2016) 531 *Nature* 591–597.

Displacement Solutions 'The Peninsula Principles on Climate Displacement within States' (2013), available at: <http://displacementsolutions.org/wp-content/uploads/2014/12/Peninsula-Principles.pdf> (last accessed 8 June 2018).

Ferris, E., 'Protection and Planned Relocations in the Context of Climate Change' (August 2012), *UNHCR Legal and Protection Policy Research Series*, PPLA/2012/04.

Freestone, D., 'International Law and Sea Level Rise' in: R.R. Churchill and D. Freestone (eds), *International Law and Global Climate Change* (London/Dordrecht: Graham & Trotman/Martinus Nijhoff, 1991), 109–125.

Freestone, D., and J. Pethick, 'Sea Level Rise and Maritime Boundaries: International Implications of Impacts and Responses', in: G. Blake (ed.) *International Boundaries: Fresh Perspectives*, Vol 5 (Routledge, 1994), 73–90.

Freestone D., and A.G. Oude Elferink, 'Flexibility and Innovation in the Law of the Sea: Will the LOS Convention Amendment Procedures Ever Be Used?' in A.G. Oude Elferink, (ed.), *Stability and Change in the Law of the Sea: The Role of the LOS Convention* (Boston/Leiden: Martinus Nijhoff, 2005) 163–216.

Freestone, D., and C. Schofield, 'Republic of the Marshall Islands: 2016 Maritime Zones Declaration Act: Drawing Lines in the Sea' (2016) 31 *International Journal of Marine and Coastal Law* 720–746.

Frost, R., et al, 'Redrawing the Map of the Pacific' (2018) 95 *Marine Policy* 302–310.

Ganopolski, A., et al, 'Critical Insolation-CO_2 Relation for Diagnosing Past and Future Glacial Inception' (2016) 529 *Nature* 200–203.

Giegerich, T., 'Article 62. Fundamental Change of Circumstances' in: O. Dörr and K. Schmalenbach (eds), *Vienna Convention on the Law of Treaties: A Commentary*, 2nd edn (Berlin: Springer, 2018), 1143–1182.

Hayashi, M., 'Sea Level Rise and the Law of the Sea – Future Options", in: D. Vidas and P.J. Schei (eds), *The World Ocean in Globalisation: Climate Change, Sustainable Fisheries, Biodiversity, Shipping, Regional Issues* (Boston/Leiden: Brill/Martinus Nijhoff, 2011) 187–206.

Human Rights Council, *Report of the Special Rapporteur on the Issue of Human Rights Obligations relating to the Enjoyment of a Safe, Clean, Healthy and Sustainable Environment*, UN Doc. A/HRC/31/52 (1 February 2016).

Institut du Droit International, Session de Hyderabad, Sixteenth Commission, 'Mass Migration', Final Resolution (9 September 2017), available at: <http://www.idi-iil.org/app/uploads/2017/08/16-RES-FINAL-EN.pdf> (last accessed 8 June 2018).

Intergovernmental Panel on Climate Change, *Climate Change 2013: The Physical Science Basis. Contribution of Working Group I to the Fifth Assessment Report of the Intergovernmental Panel on Climate Change* (Cambridge University Press, 2013).

Intergovernmental Panel on Climate Change, *Summary for Policymakers.* In: *Climate Change 2013: The Physical Science Basis. Contribution of Working Group I to the Fifth Assessment Report of the Intergovernmental Panel on Climate Change* (Cambridge University Press, 2013).

Intergovernmental Panel on Climate Change, *Summary for Policymakers*, in: *Climate Change 2014: Impacts, Adaptation, and Vulnerability, Part A: Global and Sectoral Aspects, Contribution of Working Group II to the Fifth Assessment Report of the Intergovernmental Panel on Climate Change* (Cambridge University Press, 2014).

Intergovernmental Panel on Climate Change, *Climate Change 2014: Synthesis Report. Contribution of Working Groups I, II and III to the Fifth Assessment Report of the Intergovernmental Panel on Climate Change* (Core Writing Team, R.K. Pachauri and L.A. Meyer (eds)), IPCC: Geneva, 2015.

International Law Association, Committee on Baselines under the International Law of the Sea, 'Baselines under the International Law of the Sea: Committee Report', in: International Law Association, *Report of the Seventy-Fifth Conference held in Sofia, August 2012* (London: ILA, 2012), 385–428. Available also online at <http://www.ila-hq.org/index.php/committees>.

International Law Association, *Report of the Seventy-Sixth Conference, held in Washington D.C., April 2014* (London: ILA, 2014).

International Law Association, Committee on International Law and Sea Level Rise, 'Interim Report of the Committee on International Law and Sea Level Rise', in: International Law Association, *Report of the Seventy-Seventh Conference held in Johannesburg, August 2016* (London: ILA, 2017) 842–875. Available also online at: <http://www.ila-hq.org/index.php/committees>.

International Law Commission, *Report of the International Law Commission on the Work of Its Thirty-fourth Session* (3 May–23 July 1982). General Assembly, Official Records, Thirty-seventh Session, Supplement No. 10 (UN Doc. A/37/10).

International Law Commission, Draft Articles on the Prevention of Transboundary Harm from Hazardous Activities, in: United Nations, *Report of the International Law Commission: Fifty-third Session* (21 April–1 June and 2 July–10 August 2001). General Assembly, Official Records, Fifty-sixth Session, Supplement No. 10 (UN Doc. A/56/10), 146–170.

International Law Commission, *Report of the International Law Commission: Sixty-eighth Session* (2 May–10 June and 4 July–12 August 2016). General Assembly, Official Records, Seventy-third Session, Supplement No. 10 (UN Doc. A/71/10).

International Law Commission, Draft Articles on the Protection of Persons in the Event of Disasters, in: United Nations, *Report of the International Law Commission: Sixty-eighth Session* (2 May–10 June and 4 July–12 August 2016). General Assembly, Official Records, Seventy-third Session, Supplement No. 10 (UN Doc. A/71/10), 13–73.

International Law Commission, *Report of the International Law Commission: Seventieth session* (30 April–1 June and 2 July–10 August 2018). General Assembly, Official Records, Seventy-third Session, Supplement No. 10 (UN Doc. A/73/10).

Jennings, R.Y., *The Acquisition of Territory in International Law* (Manchester University Press, 1963).

Kälin, W., and J. Künzli, *The Law of International Human Rights Protection* (Oxford University Press, 2009).

Kälin, W., 'The Human Rights Dimension of Natural or Human-Made Disasters' (2012) 55 *German Yearbook of International Law* 119–148.

Kaye, S., 'The Law of the Sea Convention and Sea Level Rise after the *South China Sea* Arbitration' (2017) 93 *International Law Studies* 423–445.

Lafferty, P., 'International migration to/from Christchurch after the Earthquakes' (PowerPoint Presentation, PANZ Conference, 29 November 2011), at <http://www.population.org.nz/wp-content/uploads/2012/02/3b3_peter-lafferty.pdf> (last accessed 8 June 2018).

Lisztwan, J., 'Stability of Maritime Boundary Agreements' (2012) 37 *Yale Journal of International Law* 153–200.

Lusthaus, J., 'Shifting Sands: Sea Level Rise, Maritime Boundaries and Inter-state Conflict' (2010) 30 *Politics* 113–118.

McAdam, J., *Climate Change, Forced Migration, and International Law* (Oxford University Press, 2012).

McAdam, J., 'Historical Cross-Border Relocations in the Pacific: Lessons for Planned Relocations in the Context of Climate Change' (2014) 49 *The Journal of Pacific History* 301–327.

McAdam, J., and E. Ferris, 'Planned Relocations in the Context of Climate Change: Unpacking the Legal and Conceptual Issues' (2015) 4 *Cambridge Journal of International and Comparative Law* 137–166.

McAdam, J., B. Burson, W. Kälin, and S. Weerasinghe, *International Law and Sea-Level Rise: Forced Migration and Human Rights*, FNI Report No. 1/2016, available at <https://www.fni.no/publications/international-law-and-sea-level-rise-forced-migration-and-human-rights-article893–290.html> (last accessed 8 June 2018).

McInerney-Lankford, A., M. Darrow and L. Rajamani, *Human Rights and Climate Change: A Review of the International Legal Dimensions* (The World Bank Group 2011).

Nansen Initiative, *Agenda for the Protection of Cross-Border Displaced Persons in the Context of Disasters and Climate Change* (Vol. I, December 2015) <https://nanseninitiative.org/wp-content/uploads/2015/02/PROTECTION-AGENDA-VOLUME-1.pdf> (last accessed 8 June 2018).

Nansen Initiative, *Agenda for the Protection of Cross-Border Displaced Persons in the Context of Disasters and Climate Change* (vol II, December 2015) <http://disasterdisplacement.org/wp-content/uploads/2015/02/PROTECTION-AGENDA-VOLUME-2.pdf> (last accessed 8 June 2018).

Office of the High Commissioner for Human Rights, *Report of the Office of the United Nations High Commissioner for Human Rights on the Relationship between Climate Change and Human Rights*, UN Doc. A/HRC/10/61 (15 January 2009).

O'Leary, M., et al, 'Ice Sheet Collapse Following a Prolonged Period of Stable Sea Level during the Last Interglacial' (2013) 9 *Nature Geoscience* 796–800.

Pratt, C., and H. Govan, *Our Sea of Islands, Our Livelihoods, Our Oceania. Framework for A Pacific Oceanscape: a catalyst for implementation of ocean policy* (Pacific Islands Forum Secretariat, November 2010), available at: <http://www.forumsec.org/wp-content/uploads/2018/03/Framework-for-a-Pacific-Oceanscape-2010.pdf> (last accessed 8 June 2018).

Prescott, J.R.V., and C. Schofield, *The Maritime Political Boundaries of the World*, 2nd edn (Leiden/Boston: Martinus Nijhoff, 2005).

Rajamani, L., 'The Changing Fortunes of Differential Treatment in the Evolution of International Environmental Law' (2012) 88 *International Affairs* 605–623.

Rayfuse, R., 'Sea Level Rise and Maritime Zones: Preserving the Entitlements of "Disappearing" States' in: M.B. Gerrard and G.E. Wannier, *Threatened Island Nations:*

Legal Implications of Rising Seas and a Changing Climate (Cambridge University Press, 2013), 167–191.

Redgwell, C., 'UNCLOS and Climate Change', (2012) 106 *American Society of International Law Proceedings* 406–409.

Rigaud, K., et al., *Groundswell: Preparing for Internal Climate Migration* (World Bank, 2018).

Rovere, A., P. Stocchi and M. Vacchi, 'Eustatic and Relative Sea Level Changes' (2016) 2 *Current Climate Change Reports* 221.

Rye, C., et al, 'Rapid Sea-level Rise along the Antarctic Margins in Response to Increased Glacial Discharge' (2014) 7 *Nature Geoscience* 732–735.

Schofield, C., 'The Trouble with Islands: The Definition and Role of Islands and Rocks in Maritime Boundary Delimitation' in: S-Y. Hong and J.M. Van Dyke (eds), *Maritime Boundary Disputes, Settlement Processes, and the Law of the Sea* (Leiden/Boston: Martinus Nijhoff, 2009) 19–38.

Schofield, C., 'Seeking Lines in the Sea: Progress and Challenges in the Delimitation of Maritime Boundaries over the Past 50 Years', in: H.N. Scheiber, N. Oral and M-S. Kwon (eds), *Ocean Law Debates: The 50-year Legacy and Emerging Issues for the Years Ahead* (Leiden/Boston: Brill/Nijhoff, 2018), 137–157.

Shepherd, A., et al, 'Mass Balance of the Antarctic Ice Sheet from 1992 to 2017' (2018) 558 *Nature* 219–222.

Soons, A.H.A., 'The Effects of a Rising Sea Level on Maritime Limits and Boundaries', (1990) 37 *Netherlands International Law Review* 207–232.

Strolazzi, C.D., et al, 'Most atolls will be uninhabitable by the mid-21st century because of sea-level rise exacerbating wave-driven flooding' (2018) 4 *Science Advances*, available online at: <http://advances.sciencemag.org/content/4/4/eaap9741>.

Thomas, A.R., 'Post-disaster resettlement in the Philippines: A risky strategy' (2015) 49 *Forced Migration Review* 52–54.

United Kingdom, The Government Office for Science, Foresight: *Migration and Global Environmental Change: Future Challenges and Opportunities: Final Project Report* (Government Office for Science, 2011), available at: <https://sustainabledevelopment.un.org/content/documents/867migrationscience.pdf> (last accessed 8 June 2018).

United Nations Committee on Economic, Social and Cultural Rights (CESCR) General Comment No 7 (1997) 'The Right to Adequate Housing, Article 11, paragraph 1, of the Covenant: Forced evictions' in Committee on Economic, Social and Cultural Rights, *Report on the Sixteenth and Seventeenth Sessions (28 April–16 May 1997, 17 November–5 December 1997)*, Economic and Social Council Official Records, 1998, Supp No 2 (E/1998/22) annex IV.

United Nations Committee on the Rights of Persons with Disabilities (CRPD), 'Concluding Observations on the Initial Report of the Czech Republic', UN Doc. CRPD/C/CZE/CO/1 (15 May 2015).

United Nations Committee on the Rights of Persons with Disabilities (CRPD), 'Concluding Observations on the Initial Report of Mauritius', UN Doc. CRPD/C/MUS/CO/1 (30 September 2015).

United Nations Committee on the Rights of Persons with Disabilities (CRPD), 'Concluding Observations on the Initial Report of Qatar', UN Doc. CRPD/C/QAT/CO/1 (2 October 2015).

United Nations Economic and Social Council, Commission on Human Rights, *Report of the Representative of the Secretary-General, Mr. Francis M. Deng, submitted pursuant to Commission Resolution 1997/39: Addendum, Guiding Principles on Internal Displacement*, UN Doc. E/CN.4/1998/53/Add.2 (11 February 1998) Introductory Note.

United Nations General Assembly, *Protection of and Assistance to Internally Displaced Persons: Note by Secretary-General* (transmitting the Report of the Special Rapporteur on the Human Rights of Internally Displaced Persons, Chaloka Beyani, in accordance with General Assembly Resolution 64/142 and Human Rights Council Resolution 14/6, UN Doc. A/66/285) (9 August 2011).

United Nations General Assembly, *One Humanity, Shared Responsibility: Report of the Secretary-General for the World Humanitarian Summit*, UN Doc. A/70/709 (2 February 2016).

United Nations High Commissioner for Refugees, Division of International Protection, 'Guidelines on Temporary Protection or Stay Arrangements' (February 2014), <http://www.refworld.org/docid/52fba2404.html> (last accessed 8 June 2018).

United Nations High Commissioner for Refugees/Georgetown University/IOM, 'A Toolbox: Planning Relocations to Protect People from Disasters and Environmental Change' (2017) <http://www.unhcr.org/596f1bb47.pdf> (last accessed 8 June 2018).

United Nations Human Rights Committee General Comment No. 29 (2001) 'Article 4: Derogations during a state of emergency', UN Doc. CCPR/C/21/Rev.1/Add.11 (31 August 2001).

Vidas, D., 'Sea Level Rise and International Law: At the Convergence of Two Epochs' (2014) 4 *Climate Law* 70–84.

Vidas, D., et al, 'International Law for the Anthropocene?' (2015) 9 *Anthropocene* 1–13.

Vidas, D., J. Zalasiewicz and M. Williams, 'What is the Anthropocene – and Why Is It Relevant for International Law?' (2015) 25 *Yearbook of International Environmental Law* 3–23.

Vidas, D., 'International Law at the Convergence of Two Epochs: Sea Level Rise and the Law of the Sea for the Anthropocene', in: H.N. Scheiber, C. Esposito, J. Kraska and M-S. Kwon (eds), *Ocean Law and Policy: 20 Years under UNCLOS* (Leiden and Boston: Brill/Nijhoff, 2017), 101–123.

Vidas, D., 'The Delimitation of the Territorial Sea, the Continental Shelf and the EEZ: A Comparative Perspective', in: A.G. Oude Elferink, T. Henriksen and S.V. Busch (eds), *Maritime Boundary Delimitation: The Case Law. Is it Consistent and Predictable?* (Cambridge University Press, 2018), 33–61.

Walker, M., et al, 'Formal Definition and Dating of the GSSP (Global Stratotype Section and Point) for the Base of the Holocene Using the Greenland NGRIP Ice Core, and Selected Auxiliary Records' (2009) 24 *Journal of Quaternary Science* 3–17.

Walker, M., et al, 'Formal subdivision of the Holocene Series/Epoch' (2012) 27 *Journal of Quaternary Science* 649–659.

Waters, C., et al, 'The Anthropocene is functionally and stratigraphically distinct from the Holocene' (2016) 351 *Science* 137.

Weil, P., *The Law of Maritime Delimitation – Reflections* (Cambridge University Press, 1989).

Weil, P., 'Geographic Considerations in Maritime Delimitation', in: J.I. Charney and L.M. Alexander (eds), *International Maritime Boundaries*, vol. 1 (Dordrecht: Nijhoff, 1993), at 115–130.

Williams, M., et al, 'The Anthropocene Biosphere' (2015) 2 *The Anthropocene Review* 196–219.

Zalasiewicz, J., P. Crutzen and W. Steffen, 'The Anthropocene', in F. Gradstein et al. (eds), *The Geologic Time Scale 2012*, Vol. 2 (Amsterdam: Elsevier, 2012), 1033–1040.

Zalasiewicz, J., et al, 'When did the Anthropocene Begin? A Mid-Twentieth Century Boundary Level is Stratigraphically Optimal' (2015) 383 *Quaternary International* 196–203.

Zalasiewicz, J., et al, 'The Working Group on the Anthropocene: Summary of evidence and interim recommendations' (2017) 19 *Anthropocene* 55–60.

Treaties and Other International Instruments

1945 Charter of the United Nations.

1948 Universal Declaration of Human Rights, UNGA res 217 A(III), 10 December 1948.

1950 Convention for the Protection of Human Rights and Fundamental Freedoms, as amended by Protocols Nos 11 and 14, supplemented by Protocols Nos 1, 4, 6, 7, 12, and 13 (European Convention on Human Rights) 213 UNTS 221.

1963 Protocol No 4 to the Convention for the Protection of Human Rights and Fundamental Freedoms, Securing Certain Rights and Freedoms Other Than Those Already Included in the Convention and in the First Protocol Thereto, as amended by Protocol No 11, ETS No 155.

1966 International Covenant on Civil and Political Rights, 999 UNTS 171.
1966 International Covenant on Economic, Social and Cultural Rights, 993 UNTS 3.
1966 International Convention on the Elimination of all Forms of Racial Discrimination, 660 UNTS 195.
1969 American Convention on Human Rights 'Pact of San José, Costa Rica', 1144 UNTS 123.
1969 Convention Governing the Specific Aspects of Refugee Problems in Africa, 1001 UNTS 45.
1969 Vienna Convention on the Law of Treaties, 1155 UNTS 331.
1970 Declaration on Principles of International Law concerning Friendly Relations and Co-operation among States in accordance with the Charter of the United Nations', UNGA res 2625 (XXV) (24 October 1970).
1971 Ramsar Convention on Wetlands of International Importance, 996 UNTS 245.
1972 Declaration of the United Nations Conference on the Human Environment (Stockholm Declaration), in *Report of the United Nations Conference on the Human Environment: Stockholm, 5–16 June 1972*, UN Doc. A/CONF.48/14/Rev.1.
1973 Agreement between Australia and Indonesia Concerning Certain Boundaries between Papua New Guinea and Indonesia, 975 UNTS 3.
1979 Convention on the Elimination of All Forms of Discrimination against Women, 1249 UNTS 13.
1980 Convention between the Government of the French Republic (Wallis and Futuna) and the Government of the Kingdom of Tonga on the Delimitation of Exclusive Economic Zones, 1183 UNTS 343.
1981 African Charter on Human and Peoples' Rights, 1520 UNTS 217.
1982 United Nations Convention on the Law of the Sea, 1833 UNTS 3.
1984 Cartagena Declaration on Refugees, adopted by the Colloquium on the International Protection of Refugees in Central America, Mexico, and Panama, 22 November 1984, in Annual Report of the Inter-American Commission on Human Rights (1984–85), OAS Doc. OEA/Ser.L/V/II.66/doc.10, rev 1, 190–93.
1985 Exchange of Notes between France and Tuvalu Constituting an Agreement Concerning Provisional Maritime Delimitation between the Two Countries, 1506 UNTS 1987.
1990 International Convention on the Protection of the Rights of All Migrant Workers and Members of Their Families, 2220 UNTS 3.
1990 United Nations, 'Humanitarian assistance to victims of natural disasters and similar emergency situations', UNGA res 45/100 (14 December 1990).
1991 United Nations, 'Strengthening of the coordination of humanitarian emergency assistance of the United Nations', UNGA res 46/182 (19 December 1991).

1992 Declaration on Environment and Development, in *Report of the United Nations Conference on Environment and Development* (Rio Declaration), Rio de Janeiro, 3–14 June 1992, A/CONF.151/26/Rev.1 (1993).

1992 United Nations Framework Convention on Climate Change, 1771 UNTS 107.

1997 Kyoto Protocol to the United Nations Framework Convention on Climate Change, 2303 UNTS 162.

2003 Treaty between Romania and Ukraine on the Romanian – Ukrainian State Border Regime, Collaboration and Mutual Assistance on Border Matters, 2277 UNTS 3.

2006 Convention on the Rights of Persons with Disabilities, 2515 UNTS 3.

2009 African Union Convention for the Protection and Assistance of Internally Displaced Persons in Africa (Kampala Convention), I-52375.

2010 The Cancún Agreements: Outcome of the work of the Ad Hoc Working Group on Long-term Cooperative Action under the Convention, in *Report of the Conference of the Parties on its sixteenth session, held in Cancun from 29 November to 10 December 2010, Addendum, Part Two: Action taken by the Conference of the Parties at its sixteenth session*, UN Doc. FCCC/CP/2010/7/Add.1 (15 March 2011).

2014 The Brazil Declaration, 'A Framework for Cooperation and Regional Solidarity to Strengthen the International Protection of Refugees, Displaced and Stateless Persons in Latin America and the Caribbean' (Brasilia, 3 December 2014), available at: <https://www.refworld.org/pdfid/5487065b4.pdf>.

2015 Paris Agreement, I-54113.

2015 Sendai Framework for Disaster Risk Reduction 2015–2030, UNGA res 69/283 (23 June 2015).

2015 Taputapuatea Declaration on Climate Change, Polynesian Leaders Group, available at: <http://www.samoagovt.ws/wp-content/uploads/2015/07/The-Polynesian-P.A.C.T.pdf>.

2016 New York Declaration for Refugees and Migrants, UNGA res 71/1 of 19 September 2016 (3 October 2016).

2017 United Nations, 'Strengthening of the coordination of emergency humanitarian assistance of the United Nations', UNGA res 71/127 (24 January 2017).

Cases, International

1969 International Court of Justice, *North Sea Continental Shelf Cases* (*Federal Republic of Germany/Denmark; Federal Republic of Germany/Netherlands*), Judgment, [1969] ICJ Reports 3.

1978 International Court of Justice, *Aegean Sea Continental Shelf* (*Greece v. Turkey*), [1978] ICJ Reports 3.

2007 *In the Matter of an Arbitration between Guyana and Suriname* (*Guyana v. Suriname*) [2007] XXX RIAA 1.

2007 International Court of Justice, *Territorial and Maritime Dispute between Nicaragua and Honduras in the Caribbean Sea (Nicaragua v. Honduras)* (Judgment) [2007] ICJ Reports 659.
2008 European Court of Human Rights, *Budayeva and Others v Russia*, App Nos 15339/02, 21166/02, 20058/02, 11673/02 and 15343/02, ECHR 2008-II.
2014 Permanent Court of Arbitration, *In the Matter of the Bay of Bengal Maritime Boundary (Bangladesh v. India)*, PCA Case 2010–16, Award of 7 July 2014.

Editors' Biographical Notes

Davor Vidas
is Research Professor in International Law and Director of the Law of the Sea Programme at the Fridtjof Nansen Institute, Norway, and Honorary Visiting Professor in the School of Geography, Geology and the Environment at the University of Leicester, UK. At the International Law Association (ILA) he has initiated, and is the Chair of, the ILA Committee on International Law and Sea Level Rise. He is a member of the Anthropocene Working Group at the International Commission on Stratigraphy. During the course of the past 25 years, he has initiated and led several major research projects on international law and interdisciplinary approaches to ocean issues, including most recently the international research project on 'Climate Change and Sea Level Rise in the Anthropocene: Challenges for International Law in the 21st Century' (Research Council of Norway, 2014–2018). Professor Vidas is the founding Editor-in-Chief of the journal monograph series *Brill Research Perspectives in the Law of the Sea* and of a popular-science book series *Anthropocene* (Školska knjiga, Zagreb).

David Freestone
is Professor of International Law and the Executive Secretary of the Sargasso Sea Commission. Within the International Law Association (ILA), he is Co-Rapporteur of the Committee on International Law and Sea Level Rise. From 1996–2008 he worked at The World Bank in Washington DC, first as head of the International and Environmental Law Practice Group, and from 2004 as Deputy General Counsel/ Senior Adviser in the Office of the General Counsel. He is Visiting Scholar/Professorial Lecturer at The George Washington University Law School in Washington DC and Associated Senior Fellow at the Fridtjof Nansen Institute in Norway and has been Professor of International Law at the University of Hull, UK. Professor Freestone has written widely on the law of the sea and international environmental law, and is the founder and Editor-in-Chief of the *International Journal of Marine and Coastal Law* (in its 34th year) and General Editor of the book series, *Legal Aspects of Sustainable*

Development, both published by Brill Nijhoff. In 2007, he received the Elizabeth Haub Gold Medal for Environmental Law.

Jane McAdam
is Scientia Professor of Law and Director of the Andrew & Renata Kaldor Centre for International Refugee Law at the University of New South Wales, Sydney, Australia. She is a Fellow of the Academy of the Social Sciences in Australia, a Research Associate at Oxford University's Refugee Studies Centre, and an Associated Senior Fellow at the Fridtjof Nansen Institute in Norway. From 2012 to 2018, Professor McAdam served as a Co-Rapporteur on the ILA Committee on International Law and Sea Level Rise. Her research has been supported by a number of Australian Research Council grants, including a prestigious Future Fellowship (2012–15). She is Editor-in-Chief of the *International Journal of Refugee Law*. In 2013, she was named a Young Global Leader by the World Economic Forum and in 2015, she was honoured as one of Australia's top ten Women of Influence, winning the 'global' category of the *Australian Financial Review* and Westpac's 100 Women of Influence awards. In 2017, she was the recipient of the prestigious Calouste Gulbenkian Prize for Human Rights.

Acknowledgments

The editors, who served as the officers – the Chair and the Co-Rapporteurs, respectively – of the ILA Committee on International Law and Sea Level Rise, wish to acknowledge the contribution of the Committee members to this Report and the related ILA Resolutions 5/2018 and 6/2018.

The comments by the reviewers and the advice provided by the Steering Committee of the 78th ILA Conference in Sydney are also gratefully acknowledged, as is the permission of the ILA to publish the Committee Report and the ILA Resolutions as a separate publication in this issue.

Finally, the support of the Research Council of Norway, within its KLIMAFORSK Programme, to the research project (no. 235638) on 'Climate Change and Sea Level Rise in the Anthropocene: Challenges for International Law in the 21st Century' (2014–2018), which facilitated the research by the editors also in preparing this report, as well as the series of inter-sessional meetings of the Committee, is gratefully acknowledged.

The Editors, 30 November 2018

www.ingramcontent.com/pod-product-compliance
Lightning Source LLC
Chambersburg PA
CBHW031331230926
51848CB00001B/192
9789004398184